Ghosts
Like
Coffee

Samantha Red Wolf

ISBN: 9781790866953

—TABLE OF CONTENTS—

Author's Note

Part 1: Stories from the Past

—AUTHOR'S NOTE—

My name is Sam.

I might not seem too unusual if you met me, but I have a knack (or I should say, *my family does)* for experiencing the *strange and unusual.*

I live in a loft apartment above my elderly mother with my two kids, one dog, two cats, six friendly, pet snakes, and a variety of mice, rats, and hamsters.

Oh, and... did I mention ghosts?

My daughter, Kiani (now twelve years old), is what you might call a psychic medium.

As far back as she can remember, she has been seeing and hearing things that would mystify and even terrify your average person.

At first, I tried to dismiss the stories she told me as being just her vivid imagination at work. But being followed around by headless and limbless floating torsos, red-eyed creatures, and corpse-like apparitions of little girls can be pretty hard to ignore.

What did I do? I researched the heck out of the subject and learned everything I could about spiritual and psychic protection.

Three years and one published book (*Ghosts Like Bacon*) about our experiences later, our house is now a lot quieter. We still get the occasional ghostly visitor (these are allowed in by our spirit guides to help them cross over) but not at the rate we used to, due to the effort we put into home protection. (See Part 3 to learn how we do it.)

The fact that the activity has slowed down is wonderful because now I can share some of my family's paranormal stories with you. There are a *lot!*

Our *new* experiences won't be left out, of course, so this book is a wonderful mixture.

Part 1 consists of all the stories from my family's past, Part 2 contains stories about my daughter and I, and Part 3 has tips on dealing with the spirit world.

I hope you enjoy these stories as much as I've enjoyed writing them.

Warm regards,
Sam

—Part 1—
Stories from the Past

—CHAPTER 1—
A CHRISTMAS RESCUE

My grandfather was born in a Cherokee Indian home built into the side of a hill in 1898. He grew up to be an Indian cowboy with a natural connection with animals and children. He had a love of stories, songs, and poems and could recite many from memory.

I remember him telling us the most incredible stories from his childhood in Oklahoma, like cowboy shoot-outs in the streets, gigantic pow wows where snake and dog were on the menu (cringe!), and even some scary encounters.

One night, many years ago, he woke up to the ghost of his abusive stepfather standing over his bed.

"You must forgive me!" his stepfather pleaded. "Please!"

When my grandfather, frozen in fear, said nothing to this, the desperate spirit then grabbed onto my grandfather's feet and began kissing them.

As you can imagine, this incident scared my grandpa so badly that even though he wasn't raised Christian (he grew up on a Cherokee Reservation until he was ten or so), he buried his head in the Bible ("The Good Book," he called it), and *made damn sure* he wouldn't encounter anything like that ever again. His determination worked—at least as far as visible entities went. Strange stuff kept happening though.

The bulk of my family's paranormal stories actually revolve around angels. This one is my favorite.

It was Christmas day in 1960. My two oldest sisters were little at this time, and I wouldn't arrive on Earth until quite a few years later.

Christmas dinner was finished, along with the pie and coffee. As was my family's habit, they decided to go for a drive around town to admire the Christmas lights. My mom and grandma felt too tired to go this time, so they stayed in hopes of getting a good nap in.

My mom was just plain exhausted after a busy day, but my grandmother, even though she hid it well, was more than just tired; she was depressed. Her relationship with my grandfather had had its ups and downs over the years, and this year was a very bad down.

Not too long after both women laid down to sleep, my mom was suddenly startled awake by an urgent voice in her head.

Get up! Your mother is trying to kill herself!

She had no idea that my grandmother was depressed and felt bewildered by this. She couldn't go back to sleep after something like that though, so she decided she would check on her mother, just to be sure.

She walked down the hall to the room where my grandma had laid down. The door was cracked open a couple inches, and my mom tip-toed up to it.

"Mother?" she called softly.

From inside the room came the sound of my grandmother's voice, tired and irritated.

"What?"

Now I suppose most people would have apologized for waking her and walked away, but my mom felt so relieved that she pushed the door open.

The room was empty.

This can't be happening. She has to be here!

My mom's desperate thought slipped her into a state of panic, and she began searching every part of the room. The bathroom, behind the curtains, and even under the bed.

Then the voice from her head spoke again.

She's in the garage with the motor running. You'd better hurry, or it will be too late.

My mom ran downstairs, threw the garage door open, and found my grandmother already unconscious.

At first, my grandma wasn't thrilled about her failed attempt, but because of how she was saved, she set aside her disbelief in God and became a believer after that.

My family believes that there were both good *and* bad forces at work that day. While one voice fought to save my grandmother, the other tried to foil the plan by getting my mother to walk away. Thank goodness, it didn't work.

—CHAPTER 2—
THE HOVERING TREE

The year was 1966.

Ever see those old films with California ranchers out herding cattle, riding horses, and skinning pigs? That was my family up until about the mid-1960s.

As babies, my mom and her sisters teethed on deer jerky. They grew up riding horses, catching lizards and horned toads, and following my grandpa just about everywhere he went.

He didn't mind either. He loved his girls so much that he used to take his babies with him to work some days. Strapped to his back with bottles and diapers, they'd have a great view over his shoulder while he worked on the roads. As they grew bigger, he would sit for hours while they braided his hair and attached little bows to each end. Sometimes, he'd give them rides on his back while he cut the lawn.

The outdoors was a way of life for my family, so it wasn't a surprise when they decided to get away from the city and live "off the grid" for a while.

The place they chose was a cabin surrounded by a beautiful forest. The property had plenty of space for trailers as well, and my family brought two of them: my grandparents' and my parents'. My oldest sisters, who were ages three to nine at the time (this was before I was born), were there as well.

One day, at lunchtime, my mom, having almost finished cooking, made a comment about getting ready to call everyone else to come and eat.

My sister, Kara, then three years old, told my mom that she would run and tell Grandpa.

She left the trailer and made her way down the hill toward Grandpa, who was busy chopping through a large tree that he planned to use to build another cabin. The path wasn't an easy one for the little girl. The forest floor held a few previously felled trees, which had to be carefully climbed over.

When Grandpa came into sight, Kara called for him, but he didn't hear her at first, so intent was he on getting through the tree.

Almost there... and... over you go, old pal.

"Grandpa!" Kara called, scrambling up and over yet another fallen tree.

My grandpa frowned.

Was that Kara's voice?

Taking his eyes off the tree, he quickly looked in the direction of the voice and spotted Kara right in the path of where the tree would soon land.

"GET OUT OF THE WAY, KARA!" he shouted. "TREE'S FALLING! DAMMIT, MOVE!"

He quickly tore his gaze from his now shocked and frozen grandchild back to the tree just as it began to fall...

Back up on the hill, the rest of the family, having heard my grandpa's desperate shouts, now watched in horror as little Kara tried to make her way back as quickly as she could over the fallen trees.

Now the whole family was shouting.

"RUN, KARA! THAT WAY! NOW!"

My mom started toward her daughter, even though she knew she wouldn't get there in time.

The heavy tree had started it's descent, and there was nothing anyone could do.

By now, Kara had made it over the last tree, but she wasn't clear yet. Instead of running left or right, which would have gotten her to safety quicker, she panicked and ran full-speed straight toward the cabin, under and along the length of the falling tree.

It seemed impossible that she would make it. But a remarkable thing happened.

Right then, halfway to the ground, the tree suddenly stopped, as if grabbed by strong, invisible hands.

And there it hovered for the time it took Kara to reach the top of the hill.

The second she was safely out of the way, the tree came down with a giant crash.

This story has been told many times over the years and was always one of my favorites. My family believes an angel saved my sister that day.

—CHAPTER 3—
VOICES

Humans are big thinkers. Our minds never stop, even when we sleep.

But sometimes, in the midst of all of these thoughts come words that are not our own.

Many people have experienced this. You don't have to be religious or even spiritual. It's been called many things: your conscience, the holy spirit, your spirit guide, your angel, God, or just your intuition.

You can be going about your business, thinking one thing or another, and suddenly, something in your mind speaks and surprises you with a bit of knowledge that hasn't occurred to you or that *you didn't even know at all*.

This has happened many times to my family and me.

My aunt once walked between two parked cars and heard *"JUMP!"* in her mind. She didn't hesitate to obey this voice, and it saved her from a collision that would surely have hurt her.

My mom sat in church one day, praying about the difficulty of her husband (my dad) being gone so often on business.

"Your husband is living a double life," a voice in her head responded.

She listened, and the voice gave her courage to transition out of a marriage that was hurting her.

I was five when I first heard *the voice*. My dad was very rarely home when I was young (which was actually a blessing, since he wasn't a kind man). I was feeling sad one day and remember praying, as my Christian mother had taught me.

(Later, in my twenties, I let go of Christianity while staying spiritual. Due to my family being part Cherokee, I resonate with a lot of native beliefs and refer to The Creator or The Source as "The Great Spirit".)

I kneeled down and poured out my feelings to The Creator and asked Him if He would be my father.

A warm feeling came over me, and in my mind, I

heard, "*YES.*"

Years later, when I was twelve, I heard *the voice* a second time.

Over the summer between third and fourth grade, I had grown from an average-height little girl to a gangly and awkward five-foot-nine. The kids at school teased me relentlessly for a long time, and though I acted like it never bothered me, *it did.*

I remember sitting in my bedroom and crying after school one day.

Why can't they accept me for my height? I thought.

Then, from my mind came words that were not my own.

"Why can't you accept yourself for your height?"

The voice and this bit of truth both startled and amazed me. I remember thinking I couldn't allow them to control me that way. I made a decision to stay positive after that.

And then, one day, *the voice* saved my life.

When I was fourteen, my best friend was a girl named Jessica. Her grandparents owned a place in the country with a few horses. When they invited me over one weekend to ride, I didn't hesitate. I missed riding. I had spent a few years in Australia learning and had even won a red ribbon in a "walk, trot, and cantor" competition.

So, when Jessica asked if I was cool with riding her second-favorite horse of the two (the first was calmer), I said, "No problem!" I felt like I could handle him.

Everything was going well for a while too, until a sudden noise startled my horse, and he took off running.

Running wasn't so bad.

But me fumbling and dropping the reins *was*.

I grabbed onto the saddle with one hand and the horse's mane with the other. I tried to grab the reins but failed. In fact, much to my horror, the horse sped up, making it nearly impossible to reach the reins without falling.

"WHOA!" I yelled. "STOP, BOY! WHOA!"

The horse ignored me and kept right on running.

All of a sudden, I was overcome by a feeling that I had to get off. *Quickly*.

Jumping from a running horse might seem easy in the movies, but I can assure you, it's not. I was terrified that I'd get caught and wind up trampled under the horse's hooves.

At that point, I became aware of the sound of Jessica behind me. She'd taken off at full speed after me and was screaming something I couldn't hear. But I could hear the terror in her voice, and it heightened mine.

I had never felt so scared. I *knew* I had to jump, but as hard as I tried, I just couldn't make myself.

After what felt like ages of hanging on, a voice in my head suddenly yelled, *"JUMP NOW!"*

This was apparently all I needed because I immediately bailed—right off of the horse—and onto the ground.

The breath was knocked out of me, but I laid there unhurt as Jessica skidded to a halt near me.

"Sam!" she cried, climbing quickly off her horse and running over to me. "Are you okay?"

I managed to nod.

"Thank God you jumped! I was so scared!"

She made a choking, crying sound, and I looked up to see her wiping at the tears on her face.

"Sam!" she went on. "There's a creek ahead with a giant rock! If you hadn't jumped, Jack would have stopped fast, and you would have gone flying right into it! It could have broken your neck!"

As I laid there trying to process this, she reached

for my hand.

"Are you okay to sit up?"

I nodded and carefully did.

When I looked at her again, she smiled with relief and then took a deep, calming breath.

"I can't believe where you landed!" she said, chuckling.

"What do you mean?" I asked her.

Jessica explained how her grandpa had started a building project here and then just left it. All the large rocks and sharp sticks in the ground under me had been removed.

Not only had I been saved by a *voice* in my head, but the voice had even timed my jump so that I would land *right in the softest patch of dirt for miles.*

—CHAPTER 4—
THE MAN WITH THE TWISTED FACE

The most terrifying paranormal encounter of my life happened when I was sixteen.

My sister, Kara, was in town visiting us, and I'd fixed my bedroom up for her. There were only two bedrooms in our upstairs condominium, but we had a comfy sofa and my mom's bed was a queen, so I had the option to sleep in her bed as well.

That night, I had stayed out late with a good friend of mine named James. We'd gone to a party, got bored, and decided we would just drive around and talk, which we were good at. James and I could talk for hours about almost anything.

That night, the subject was the existence of God. James was convinced that He didn't exist, and I was convinced He did.

We became so involved in discussing theories

and analyzing experiences that we actually pulled over to the side of the road to focus better.

While we sat there talking, I suddenly became aware of a feeling of being watched. It wasn't a neutral kind of feeling either. It felt hostile and too close for comfort. Ever heard that phrase, "breathing down the back of your neck"? That's what it felt like.

I tried to ignore it, but it was hard. Then I noticed that James was behaving strangely. He would sometimes stop mid-sentence, look behind him, and rub the back of his neck before continuing.

After a few times of this, I outright asked him about it.

"Do you feel really weird right now; like someone is watching us?"

His response came fast.

"Yes! It's freaking me out! Do you?"

"Yes!"

"Let's get out of here," he suggested.

"Good idea."

When we arrived at my house, we said our goodbyes, and I ran upstairs to get ready for bed.

The sofa was comfy, and it wasn't long before I'd drifted off.

Sometime in the middle of the night, a sound startled me awake.

I remember sitting up and noticing that the TV remote now lay on the floor (it had been on the armrest of the sofa by my feet). I naturally assumed my foot had knocked it off, and I shrugged, laid back down, and closed my eyes.

I expected to continue the nonsensical dream I'd been having but I was amazed when I saw my living room instead.

It looked just as the room would look if my eyes had been open, except I knew that they weren't.

I stared wonderingly around me starting with the fireplace, then the TV set, the window, a chair, the front door, and finally, the end of the sofa, where the view of my mother's bedroom door was blocked by the body of a man.

He sat on the armrest by my feet, facing away from me. His hair was brown and cut short, and he had a pair of jeans on but no shirt.

As I lay there staring at him, he slowly stood up and turned around.

His body might have looked normal, but his face was horrifying. His features were twisted and moved continuously, as if he were trying to form a proper face and couldn't.

Rage emanated from him like cold mist out of an icebox. With it came a freezing wind, blowing out from his body and over mine.

"You stupid bitch!" he screamed at me. "Stop talking to James about God, or I'll kill you."

I stared in shocked horror as he began walking toward me, around the sofa.

"Better yet, I'll disembowel your useless family and make you watch."

This was too much for me. I broke free of the "nightmare" by shaking my head, but when I opened my eyes, the only thing that had changed was that the man's body had vanished.

I could still hear him screaming at me, and the icy wind kept right on blowing. With it came a heavy pressure on my chest, as if someone were sitting on it.

I gasped and tried to scream and sit up but failed at both. Whatever this thing was, it had no intention of letting me speak or move.

Desperately trying to think what to do, I suddenly recalled my mom once saying to use the name of Jesus Christ if I ever encountered a demon. Since I did not believe in ghosts at this time, I could only assume that that was what this thing was.

I tried to speak Jesus's name, but all that came out of my mouth was air.

Please, God, I thought. *Give me my voice.*

I kept trying to speak, and finally, my voice grew stronger.

"IN THE NAME OF JESUS CHRIST, I COMMAND YOU TO LEAVE MY HOUSE! NOW!"

The reaction was immediate.

The spirit screamed in rage and frustration. The wooden blinds over the window banged loudly against the glass and then went still. Then the wind died down and stopped. Everything was calm once more.

I sat up easily then. My cheeks were wet with tears I hadn't been aware of crying as I ran quickly into my mom's room, to tell her what had happened.

As you can imagine, this experience has never left my mind.

Many years and much experience later, I'm still not sure what this entity was, but I do have a theory. If it was really a demon—or "dark one" as I now call them—why did it take the form of a shirtless man? Why not take one of the more menacing shapes these entities seem to favor? My daughter says the ones she's seen never look human, and why would they? Fear is the energy they crave and feed upon, so why appear to be human at all?

It seems likely to me, considering everything, that this spirit had probably known James (and possibly myself) before he'd died and had attempted to hide his features from me. I think he had been getting his energy needs met by soaking in James's occasional bouts of teenage anger. My attempts at upping my friend's vibes and therefore souring the spirit's energetic meal was not something he was going to put up with.

—CHAPTER 5—
THE CURSE

The man with the twisted face wasn't the only dark spirit encounter of my teenage years. A year or so later, I was visited by not one but *twelve* of these beings in a single night. It was so disturbingly strange that I would have doubted my senses if it weren't for the fact that my mother experienced it with me.

When I was seventeen, I had a boyfriend for a couple months, Paul, whom I spent a lot of time with. He was a lot of fun to talk to and be around in general. Things didn't go well for long, however. When Paul started hanging out with a gang of skinheads, my fondness turned to disgust, and I dumped him.

He wasn't too happy about this and complained to anyone who would listen.

After yet another night of avoiding Paul's presence at my favorite hang-outs, I went home and climbed into bed, exhausted and more than ready for a good night's sleep.

Just as I was starting to drift off, I suddenly became aware of the feeling of being watched.

At first, I tried to blame my paranoia on too much caffeine, but I'd gone to bed sleepy, so that didn't make sense.

I tried my best to ignore the feeling and go to sleep anyway, but the harder I tried, the more aware I became.

It wasn't just *one* thing watching me. It felt like *twelve very hateful things,* and the fact that the number felt so precise worried me even more.

Am I staying up too late these days? Maybe sleep deprivation and drinking so much coffee is affecting my head.

I thought about rebuking the things out loud, like I'd done with the twisted man, but part of me felt like I was being ridiculous.

Twelve evil spirits in my room? Not possible. Maybe a change of scenery will snap me out of this.

I got up and made my way to my mom's bedroom.

As I mentioned in my first book, I had suffered from terrible nightmares since I was a little girl. They didn't stop until after my daughter was born, when we learned about burning sage and the many other useful ways of keeping the home clear of negative energy.

My mom knew about my nightmares and always said I was welcome to sleep with her on those nights. I often did, and it usually helped.

Not this time though.

"You okay?" my mom asked when she felt me climb into the bed.

Not wanting to worry her, I replied with, "Yeah, I'm fine. Just had a nightmare."

"Oh, okay. Night, honey."

"Night, Mom."

I laid down and closed my eyes, but it wasn't long before I realized that nothing had changed. Whatever those things were, they'd followed me in here.

Crap. Now what? Should I wake her up and tell her what's going on? I don't want to upset her. I should handle this on my own.

I was thinking over the best way to handle it

when my mom woke up again.

"What's wrong?"

"Nothing's wrong, Mom. Go back to sleep."

"All right."

What in the world? Does she sense them too? Maybe I should just pray about it in my mind. Would that work?

I was going over what to say when my mom suddenly jerked awake.

"GET OUT!" she snapped.

I turned to look at her, alarmed.

"OUT! GET OUT!"

Her arm shot out of the covers as if she were pushing something away from her.

"What's wrong?" I exclaimed.

"Something just lifted the covers up and tried to climb in!"

I stared at her, wide-eyed.

"What's going on?" she demanded. "I *knew* something wasn't right. Tell me right now."

She sat up and took my hand.

With the cat quite definitely out of the bag at this point, I explained what I'd felt in my bedroom and how I'd also felt them follow me.

She listened and nodded and then we held hands

and prayed together.

The dark spirits left quickly.

Though I was relieved, I also felt disturbed. Exactly *how* had such a thing happened? What had caused it?

Three days later, I was hanging out with a friend when a guy I knew approached me with an odd look on his face.

"I debated about whether I should tell you this or not," he said, biting his lip and looking around him before continuing. "But I figured you should know. I overheard Paul bragging that he'd talked this witch chick into putting a curse on you."

When I expressed shock over this and asked him what night Paul had hung with the witch girl, he'd said three days ago.

I was stunned. This was the same night that the twelve dark spirits had come into my room.

Well, I'll be damned. There was the answer to my question.

I thought about confronting Paul after this, but I didn't want to get the guy who had come to me in trouble. Finally, I decided to just pray about the situation. It must have worked because I didn't encounter another dark one until years later.

—CHAPTER 6—
THE BALCONY

When my son was one year old, *the voice* saved his life. He doesn't remember, of course, but I will never forget it.

My son's nickname is Happy (Hap for short). We call him this not only to honor my grandfather, who had the same nickname, but also because he *is happy,* almost constantly. I've never known a more laid-back, gentle, happy soul in my entire life, and turning fifteen hasn't put one dent in him.

There's only one thing that will make Hap mad, and that's his little sister. Kiani *loves* to play practical jokes on him. He takes it in stride most of the time, but her creative joke projects would test the patience of a saint.

When Hap was one, we lived in an upstairs apartment. Being a new mother and having longed for children more than anything, I was always worried about every little thing. I had the place baby-proofed from one end to the other, including the sliding glass door leading out to the upstairs balcony, which was directly above a cement walkway. I'd found a white rod that fit right in the sliding track of the door, and it looked almost invisible unless you were looking for it. Hap had tried opening the door a few times without success, and seeming oblivious as to why, he always walked off and forgot about it.

I underestimated him though.

One day, I was sitting at my computer across the room from the sliding door. I was very involved in what I was doing and failed to notice Hap making his way toward the door yet again.

Suddenly, an urgent voice filled my head.

"Hap is on the balcony!"

I don't think I've ever moved that quickly. I was out of the chair and across the room in a flash.

And there was my baby on the balcony, standing on a plastic chair, trying to climb onto the railing.

I snatched him up fast and held him to me, my heart pounding in my chest. My head filled with gratitude beyond words.

"Thank you!" I whispered. "Thank you!"

—CHAPTER 7—
KIANI

My longing to have children started when I was still a kid. I used to tell the adults around me that I would one day have two kids: first a boy and then a girl (which is exactly what I had!).

Imagine my dismay, in my twenties, when I couldn't conceive. We tried for five years but to no avail. I wanted children *so* bad that I even experienced a couple false pregnancies (where your body has all the symptoms).

I remember the depression I felt during that time. It was awful.

My prayers to The Great Spirit did not go unheard, however. In fact, children would be a big part of the plan He had for me.

One day, on a whim, I decided to stop eating artificial colors, flavors, and additives. The effect was incredible!

I dropped sixteen pounds in two months, lost the majority of my health problems, and became pregnant with my son.

There never was a happier pregnant woman. I didn't even experience much nausea or anything else uncomfortable, other than the baby kicking me a little too hard at times.

Later, when Hap was two years old, I remember being hit by a powerful urge to become pregnant again. It was literally all I thought about. Looking back on it and knowing the destiny ahead for my daughter and myself, it was truly no wonder.

When I became pregnant with Kiani, I knew instantly, the same day I conceived.

"You can't know that!" my mom exclaimed when I told her.

"I know it sounds nuts, but I know. I *feel* it!"

I put my hands on my stomach and was amazed yet again at the energy I felt there.

"Just wait," I said. "You'll see."

When I missed my period, I tested myself. It was a strong positive, and with the knowledge came a sudden flash of an image in my mind. It was like being shown a photograph, and it lasted maybe three or four seconds.

In it was the smiling face of a one-year-old little girl. She had brown hair; dark, chocolate brown eyes, like my own; and eyes shaped like my husband's. Her hair was still growing and rather sparse in the front, and it was tied up in two adorable top knots with little bows. (I assure you that she looked *exactly* like this at age one, even down to the top knots. I remember trying to leave her hair alone in the front, but it looked so odd being that sparse that I had no choice but to tie it up.)

This photograph-like flash both startled and enchanted me beyond measure. I had never experienced anything like that before, but I didn't question it. I *knew* this was the baby I was carrying.

That wasn't the only amazing premonition I got during this time. When I had an ultrasound done and found out that I did indeed carry a little girl, I went home for a nap and had a dream.

In it was an older version of the little girl I saw in my head. She was about nine years old and was chattering happily at me as we walked through a grocery store. In the dream, she was giving her opinion on everything I picked out and reminding me to check labels for additives. I remember thinking, *What a strong personality this girl has!* And I can tell you, she is exactly like the girl in my dream to this day! She is quiet around strangers but will talk the ears off anyone she knows, and if there's room for an opinion on something, she has one—or even several.

The increase in intuitive abilities while I was pregnant with Kiani was pretty amazing. I am naturally a *little* psychic but not to the extent I was when I was pregnant with my daughter. The abilities that I already possessed increased, and with them came one or two I didn't even have.

Some of what I experienced was an increase in claircognizance (knowing random bits of information without knowing why), telepathic impressions (random thoughts from my mother or husband), clairsentience (psychic feeling of the emotions, physical sensations, and energy around you) and procognition (seeing or dreaming of events that haven't happened yet.) It's my opinion that my daughter's psychic abilities amplified mine while I carried her.

Most of what I experienced was fairly trivial, but my favorite of this time period was when I woke up one day with an overwhelming desire for a fried peanut butter and banana sandwich. I'd never had one before and didn't even know what it tasted like, but I *had to have one.*

Didn't Elvis used to eat these things? I remembered thinking as I slid the piping hot sandwich onto a plate and grabbed a napkin.

My mouth was watering as I headed toward my computer desk.

I set the plate down on my lap, took a bite out of my sticky, sweet breakfast, then turned my computer on.

When I opened the internet browser, I almost dropped my sandwich. There at the top of the page, were the words, *"HAPPY BIRTHDAY, ELVIS!"*

—CHAPTER 8—
THE TELEPORTING WALLET

When Kiani was around nine months old, I came home from a trip to the mall to discover that my wallet had gone missing.

In my desperation, I must have searched through my diaper bag at least four times. I even went so far as to take each individual item out of the bag and lay them across the sofa. No wallet.

I checked the car. No wallet.

Then I called the places I'd been to. No wallet.

I didn't want to, but it looked as if I would have no choice but to call the bank, cancel my cards, replace them, *and* get a new driver's license.

I remember feeling like I could cry. The kids and the housework kept me very busy, and now I had to take time to replace everything I'd lost *and* couldn't even drive myself to the grocery store.

I prayed about it before heading off to bed, hoping that by some miracle, it could still be found.

That night, as I lay fast asleep, I was suddenly startled awake by an image "dropped" into my head. It was my diaper bag.

I laid there feeling baffled for a minute, then fell back asleep.

Then it happened again. An image of my diaper bag appeared so strongly in my mind that it woke me up.

What the heck?

I sat up this time and slid my feet to the floor.

All right, Great Spirit, I thought. *Is this your way of telling me to check my bag again, or am I losing my mind?*

Feeling kind of silly but unable to resist the hope, I stood up and made my way to the living room, where my bag sat, still on the sofa.

I opened it up and reached in. On the top sat a little baggie of baby snacks, which I pulled out and set aside.

I reached in again, and my hand immediately closed around a very familiar object. I gasped and pulled it out.

I imagine I must have looked a bit like Indiana

Jones standing there, my face a mixture of awe and amazement as I stared at the priceless relic in my hand. It was unmistakably and without a doubt... my missing wallet.

—CHAPTER 9—
DR. GREAT SPIRIT

When Kiani was two years old, she began breaking out in hives for no reason that I could discern. Her intestines weren't happy either and expressed this by refusing to release her food in solid form.

The doctor didn't know what was wrong with her, and even the alternative healer I visited had no clue. She suggested that I put her on a very strange and difficult diet, which I can't recall the details of.

I followed her advice and saw no results after two days. I became worried and prayed several times a day, hoping for an answer.

I didn't have long to wait.

One day, a voice inside my head spoke to me. *"Feed her the foods that I intended for her, and she will not be ill."*

I have to admit to being stupidly puzzled by this at first and didn't react right away. I kept on with the weird diet for another day or two.

But The Great Spirit didn't give up. Three more times, He repeated the same phrase in my head: *"Feed her the foods that I intended for her, and she will not be ill."*

Suddenly, in my head, I saw a garden. Out of it grew vegetables and trees with fruit. I also saw rice and grains growing, and it hit me.

Organic foods!

I thanked The Great Spirit for helping me and especially for not giving up when I wasn't listening.

I had been avoiding additives for years, but I realized that I had been making exceptions with some foods because the kids liked them so much. That had been my mistake. I tossed everything in my kitchen that wasn't 100% organic, pure, or non-GMO into charity bags and went shopping.

The next morning, Kiani's hives had vanished as well as her tummy problems.

I was so grateful! There is no better doctor than The Creator.

—CHAPTER 10—
THE TOWER

When Hap was six and Kiani three, we moved to North Carolina, where I live to this day.

Some of the most amazing things happened to us at that time.

The most astounding for me was the night my son "eavesdropped" on a dream I was having.

As I mentioned in *Ghosts Like Bacon*, our bedroom setup wasn't really standard by western culture. Though the kids had their own rooms, I never forced them to sleep alone, opting instead to place two gigantic Japanese-style mattresses laid back-to-back so that we could all sleep in the same room if we wanted to. No falling out of bed, no baby monitors, and no staggering from my bedroom at two a.m. to the call of a crying child.

It was my habit at this time to lay down with my kids for a few minutes at bedtime before getting up to watch a movie downstairs.

I was very tired that night, however, and soon fell asleep and into a dream.

It was rather nonsensical, as half of my dreams tend to be. One thing odd about it though was that the dream played out *below* me, as if I were a cameraman filming the scene from up high.

It was nighttime, and I saw a man on a bicycle peddling down a side street. It began to rain, and he sped up quickly, coming to a hard stop at a wooden fence. He climbed off the bike, leaned it against the fence, opened the gate, and ran across the yard to the house.

I remember being somewhat startled at the sight of it. It wasn't a house. It was a tower.

It was made entirely of red brick, with the occasional window on each story and a sliding glass door on the bottom back side, overlooking a concrete patio.

As the man approached the building, the outside lights turned on, and the sliding glass door opened. A woman stood there.

What followed was a rather odd conversation.

"I didn't know you were coming," said the woman.

"You should have left the light on," replied the man.

"Well, you should have worn louder tennis shoes," countered the woman.

Suddenly, the sound of Hap's voice woke me, and my eyes snapped open.

His face was less than a foot from my own, and though he was obviously fast asleep, his lips parted and he said in a clear voice, "You should have worn tennis shoes louder."

If anyone had been awake to see the look on my face, I'm positive it would have been a comical one.

With the exception of the two switched words, Hap had repeated the man's words exactly! I was completely amazed!

I couldn't wait to tell their dad about it, so I got up and slipped quietly out of the room. I made my way downstairs.

There was a light on in the office, and I could see him sitting at his computer, staring thoughtfully at the screen.

As I approached, he turned to me, and my eyes slid from his face to his computer.

I stopped, my mouth falling open in shock yet *again*.

There, displayed in full color on his browser, was an image of a *red brick tower!*

—CHAPTER 11—
THE INVISIBLE HUG

The death of a pet can be devastating. I've lost many furry friends over the years, but my cat, Shadow, was one of the hardest for me, probably because of how pure and wise his soul seemed to be. He had these bright gold eyes that seemed to look right through you, as if he had a direct link to The Great Spirit.

I met him one day while visiting the animal shelter. My elderly cat, Misha, was dying. I hoped that bringing another cat into our home might be a good distraction for me and help keep the tears from coming quite so often.

The shelter was unusual in the fact that instead of using cages, they kept all their cats in one giant room. It was quite a sight! There must have been over seventy cats in that room. They were just hanging out, some sleeping, some playing, some eating, and some staring out the windows.

When I walked in, many of them took notice of me, and a few ran over to greet me.

I sat down on the floor and immediately became a "cat couch" as at least ten cats surrounded me for pets and cuddles.

One little cat in particular, who had a broken tail, decided I was the bee's knees and would swat at the other cats, as if to say, *"This one's mine! Back off!"*

As I sat there enjoying all the feline attention, I looked up and noticed a black cat sitting off to the side, watching me.

He startled me a bit because not only were his eyes the most beautiful shade of gold, but he seemed to possess this other-worldly wisdom. It radiated out from those glorious eyes, and he gazed at me as if he already knew me. If cats could smile, he would have been.

"Ah, there you are," he seemed to say. *"I've been expecting you."*

I called to him, but he didn't approach me. He just looked at me as if he thought I was marvelous and was perfectly content to just watch me for the time being.

I sat there for another twenty minutes or so, enjoying all the cats' headbutts, purrs, meows, and chirps. Then the door opened, and one of the volunteers walked in.

She smiled at the sight of me surrounded by so many cats and asked if there was one I was interested in.

"Actually," I replied, standing up and brushing some of the cat hair off my lap and legs, "there are two cats I'm interested in, but I can't decide on which one."

I smiled sheepishly at her, and she laughed kindly.

"Aww, which ones?"

"This little cat here, with the broken tail, and that one there, black with gold eyes."

"Well, no wonder you're having trouble! Those two are little dolls. You have great taste."

I smiled.

"Do you need some more time to decide?"

I looked back and forth between the two and finally said, "I guess I'll go with the broken-tailed one. He definitely seems to like me."

The lady glanced down at the broken-tailed cat,

who was winding himself around and around my legs, purring like a little car, and laughed.

"Okay," she chuckled. "I'll get his paperwork and be right back."

A while later, she returned with a confused expression on her face.

"This is the strangest thing," she began, shaking her head. "We can't find his paperwork anywhere. This never happens. We are very organized here."

I assured her that it was okay and not to stress too much over it.

"I know that you were really hoping to adopt today," she continued. Her gaze was sympathetic as I had told her about my cat, Misha. "Maybe you could take the black cat home today instead, just for now, and when we find the missing paperwork, we can call you."

I glanced at the black cat, who hadn't moved one inch from the spot he'd been in. I wasn't surprised, somehow, to see him still gazing at me. It was as if we'd been best friends for years, and I'd finally come to pick him, like he knew I would.

I smiled and nodded. "Okay, let's do that," I replied.

As you can imagine, I never did trade him in for

the broken-tailed cat.

Once home, I set the cat carrier down and opened the door. He stepped out, looked left and right, spotted the stairs, and without another thought, went straight upstairs and down the hall to the bathroom, where Misha was laying on a blanket.

I followed him and watched in awe as he padded silently up to her, touched her nose with his own, and laid down alongside her.

A few days went by, and not once did Shadow leave that bathroom. We called to him, tried to lure him out with treats and cat food, but he wouldn't eat any of it unless we set it down on the bathroom floor.

He used the litter box a few feet away and ate normally, but the majority of his time was spent curled up right alongside Misha.

Sadly, my sweet girl passed away a little more than a week later. It was a sad time for me, but Shadow's presence was like a warm light in a dark tunnel.

With Misha now gone, Shadow finally emerged from the upstairs bathroom and made his way downstairs.

He inspected every corner of the house and rubbed up against us in passing as if to say, "*Hey, fam. Sorry it took me a while. I had something I needed to do.*"

Shadow continued to amaze me over the next three years. He was so laid-back and sweet and possessed the patience of a monk when it came to my overly-enthusiastic puppy, Luna, and one-year-old Kiani, who kept picking him up at every opportunity.

Luna loved to wrestle, and Shadow would patiently allow it. He played with her for hours until they would both plop down, exhausted.

Kiani would pick Shadow up upside-down, and he would just hang there, like a wet noodle, waiting for her to put him back down again.

Needless to say, I adored him beyond measure. I just wish I'd known how short my time with him would be.

Only one year after we moved to North Carolina, Shadow came down with a rare blood disease caused by a mosquito bite. The bacteria robbed his body of oxygen, and though the doctor and I fought desperately to save him, it was all for nothing. He passed away in my arms on the way to the veterinary hospital.

His death felt like the death of a child to me. Feeling like my heart had been torn from my chest, I cried and cried for days and days. I cried so much and so often that I would wake up to my pillow soaked in tears.

The only thing that seemed to distract me was writing. I hadn't written a thing in years and had pretty much given up on myself in that area. So many unfinished novels had made me feel like a failure. But I was desperate, and it was the only thing I could think of that was so involving that it could make me forget where I was. So, I set aside my reservations. I started on some short stories, and much to my relief, it did help me.

When nighttime came, though, the tears would return.

On one particularly bad night, I remember lying in bed and pleading with The Great Spirit to ease my grief.

"It hurts so much!" I sobbed. "I don't know what to do to make it stop."

Suddenly, I felt a presence behind me. I didn't look and didn't wonder because I knew instantly what it was from the tremendous feeling of love and peace that filled the air around me.

It was a guardian spirit, an angel.

And what happened next, I will *never forget*.

I felt this beautiful light being wrap its arms around me and hold me.

I remember marveling at the fact that though I couldn't see arms around me or feel a body behind me, the energy of the hug was no less real. In fact, I can truthfully say that was the best hug I've ever had.

My tears stopped instantly, and I fell asleep completely enveloped in those invisible, loving arms.

Nine years later, I sometimes think back on that time in my life and I remember how lost and sad I felt—and not just over Shadow's death. I know in my heart that everything happens for a reason, and I feel that his death was not in vain. If he hadn't died, I might never have started writing again—and *that* might very well have been Shadow's gift to me and why he seemed to be *not of this world*.

Thank you, my little friend. I can't wait to see you again one day.

—CHAPTER 12—
SAFER TRAVELS

Driving a car. It's such a major part of our lives that we can sometimes forget that we are traveling at tremendous speeds with nothing but a little steel and plastic to keep our delicate bodies safe.

I've always been fascinated by stories of people being saved by invisible forces—and most especially by those involving cars.

My favorite is one my sixth-grade teacher told me. He said he'd been driving on a fast-moving road when a car going the opposite direction suddenly crashed through the center divide and headed straight toward him. My teacher was surrounded by other cars and had nowhere to move to avoid the collision. He said he knew he was going to die and braced for the impact. But instead of hitting him, the approaching car *drove right through him* and out the other side, as if my teacher and his car were nothing but mist. That story amazed me. I never forgot it.

Though my experiences are not quite as dramatic as my teacher's, they are still remarkable to me.

The first one happened a few months after moving to North Carolina. I had both kids in the backseat and was getting ready to pull out of my neighborhood and onto the main road when something really bizarre happened. My truck's left wheels suddenly lifted up off the ground and came back down, followed by the same thing from the right side.

It definitely got my attention, and I stopped the truck.

"Did we hit something?" Hap asked, worried.

"I don't know," I replied. "Stay there and keep your seatbelt on. I'm going to check."

I turned the ignition off, got out, and walked around the truck. There was absolutely nothing under it, behind it, or even in front of it. The road was entirely clear of objects, and we'd long passed the nearest speed bump.

I stood there baffled for a few moments, then climbed back into the truck.

"What was it?" the kids asked me.

"Nothing was there," I replied. "That was the weirdest thing! It felt like someone lifted the truck!"

"Like a giant!" said Hap.

"Could have been an angel," three-year-old Kiani piped in.

I turned to her and smiled.

"Could be," I told her, not putting much thought into it.

Once back on the road, though, I couldn't help but wonder. Lifting my truck for no apparent reason didn't mean there *wasn't a reason*. What exactly had I avoided by not pulling out onto the road at that time? Had we been saved from a potential car accident? I'm positive I'll find out one day.

The second incident came about three years later, while I was out shopping with Kiani.

The store parking lot was packed near the entrance. Not wanting to deal with the crowds, I decided to park way out at the end, away from all the chaos. There wasn't a car near us in either direction.

Once out of the truck, I took Kiani's hand and turned toward the store.

Suddenly, from behind us, came the sound of someone walking.

We turned to see a woman, who smiled at us.

"You'd better check the air on that back tire," she said, pointing toward my truck. "It can be dangerous when it gets that low."

"Oh, thank you!" I replied.

She smiled again in return and kept walking. I made my way quickly to the back of the truck. The tire was indeed very low.

When I looked up, Kiani was turning from me to where the woman had been.

"Where'd she go?" she asked me.

I moved my gaze upward and saw what she meant. The woman who had spoken to us was nowhere in sight. She couldn't have made it to the store or even the other side of the parking lot that quickly.

I looked the other direction and saw nothing but empty parking places. Where was her car? Where had she come from?

Again, Kiani was quick to offer her opinion.

"That lady was probably an angel, Mommy," she said in this sweet, knowing voice.

I took her hand and nodded, glancing once more behind me at the empty parking lot.

"I think you're right," I replied.

—Part 2—
Stories from the
Present

—CHAPTER 13—
THE HOUSE FAIRY

*F*airies.

We might believe in them as children, but like most everyone, I had decided years ago that they were just wishful fantasy.

However, when you have a child who can see the spirit world and other similar dimensions, one can't help but be a little open-minded, especially considering some of the things Kiani and I have experienced. This experience, though, was something entirely new.

As I've mentioned before, Kiani sleeps in my room at night and has since she was a baby. Who can blame her with the things she sees?

It was about ten in the evening, and all my bedroom lights were off, except for the gentle glow of my salt lamp.

Kiani said I had fallen asleep and was actually snoring a little, which only happens when I'm truly exhausted. Not the least bit sleepy yet, Kiani had her tablet out and was playing on it while I slept.

Soon, she started to become aware of some odd sounds coming from the little, square-shaped wall shelf to her left, which held the miniscule remains of a granola bar and an empty plastic cup. She said she heard the granola bar wrapper crinkling, followed by tiny footsteps, then crunching sounds, then a happy sigh and what can only be described as tiny "mmm"-like sounds of appreciation.

Feeling both disturbed and curious, Kiani slowly sat up and peered into the shelf. There, she saw a tiny, human-like figure. Having suddenly noticed her, it quickly ran behind the cup and hid, bumping the cup forward a bit in its haste to not be seen.

I woke up shortly after this to find her wide-eyed and anxious.

"Mommy, that was really freaky," she said after explaining what she'd seen. "What *was* that? Do you think it was a fairy?"

"Sounds a lot like a fairy to *me*," I replied. "Actually, it sounds *exactly like a brownie.*"

"What is *that?*"

"It's a wingless fairy, kind of like a tiny elf. They like human houses and will come inside and make themselves at home. Supposedly, they chase off scary-looking spiders, and if they like you, they'll help you find missing items."

"Whoa..."

"Yeah. Also, they love gifts of food, especially sweet stuff like cookies and honey."

"No wonder he liked that granola bar, then."

I laughed. "Yep. Especially considering those *yum-yum* sounds he made. Maybe we should keep leaving him treats in that same spot."

Kiani's eyes widened.

"Yeah! Oh! I know what else too! I can put my little toad house from outside on that shelf. Think he'll like that?"

"I'm sure he will."

I was thoughtful for a while before falling back asleep. Kiani has seen many spirits and unexplained phenomena over the years but had never seen a nature spirit until now. Why was that?

Then it dawned on me. *The staurolite!* Otherwise known as "the fairy cross", this protective stone is also known to increase your ability to see nature spirits of various kinds. I hadn't owned any until a couple months ago, when I decided to buy two new protective crystals. Kiani had been wearing one around her neck every day.

I suspected this wouldn't be a solitary encounter, and I was right. Kiani has seen so many brownies since that we are starting to learn their habits and their general appearances. They range anywhere from five to eight inches in height, and they have brown or black hair (some are bald), long arms and legs, and pointed ears.

Though some brownies don't wear clothing (YouTube "Mum films weird goblin-like creature" and check out the video; Kiani says this is definitely a real brownie caught on film but without clothing), ours are always clothed in tiny, badly-sewn outfits made from (we're assuming) whatever they can find lying about. Some even wear tiny (also badly sewn) hats, like Santa's elves.

They are mostly nocturnal and are expert climbers. I can't say I blame them for this habit as the floor seems a dangerous place for something so little. Almost every time she's spotted one, they are either climbing a shelf, running across one, or peeking around objects placed on shelves.

Once, when I was doing some healing energy

work on Kiani, one of them became curious and jumped from a bookshelf to my shoulder to get a better look at what I was doing. I didn't feel the sensation of him on my shoulder, but I wasn't trying to either, as I've done with animal spirits.

A few days after this, Kiani looked up to see one climbing a bookshelf in my bedroom. I was surprised to see movement when I looked as well, so I quickly snapped a photo. I was not expecting to catch anything, but to my delighted surprise, a tiny, mist-colored face could be seen standing next to a candle. It had slanted eyes, pointed ears, and a mischievous little smile.

I'm not sure if he meant for us to see him, but just in case—and as a reward—I left him a little bowl of honey and oats next to the candle.

I can honestly say that I'm truly enjoying having these little guys around. It's opened me up to a whole new realm of possibilities, and I'm excited to learn more about the world of the fae.

And if you're wondering if you might have a brownie or two in your house, I can assure you that you just might! But take heed, curious human.

Legend says that although brownies bring luck and prosperity to the homes they live in, they can turn mischievous rather quickly if you are cruel or attempt to hurt them. Outrageous messes in the kitchen and missing prized objects are their way of getting revenge before leaving your home forever.

—CHAPTER 14—
THE STRANGER THINGS

One might imagine that the spirits Kiani sees are made up of human and animal spirits, angels, and a few fairies. You wouldn't be wrong, but there are also some *very* strange beings as well. In this chapter, I'll touch on a few of these. If you're easily disturbed, I would skip this part.

1. EXTRATERRESTRIALS

Kiani has seen a few spirits that seem to fall into this category. I've even looked up information on some of the lesser-known ones and found that, according to many, they *do* exist—at least in theory.

The fact that extraterrestrials appear in The Spirit Realm is interesting to me and brings up questions. Are they spirits of extraterrestrials, or do extraterrestrials have the ability to slip in and out of The Spirit Realm?

I've read some books that say there are hundreds of dimensions running parallel to our own.[1] Our human eyes can't see into these dimensions because they vibrate at vastly different frequencies than our own. It's said that ETs know how to use these dimensions to observe us without being noticed. These dimensions also serve to protect the ETs from the uncomfortable, lower frequencies of our planet.

Many of these beings are not only more technologically advanced than us; they are also more spiritually advanced as well. Imagine how yucky it

---

[1] If you're curious to know more about ETs, check out Dolores Cannon's books—*The Custodians: Beyond Abduction; Keepers of Garden*; *The Convoluted Universe* series; *The Legend of Starcrash*; and *The Three Waves of Volunteers and the New Earth*. Dolores Cannon is a best-selling author, past-life regressionist and hypnotherapist who specialized in the recovery and cataloging of lost knowledge. Having started her work in 1979, her experience and hypnotherapy techniques were then passed on through her classes and her books. Her legacy, knowledge, and tools continue to grow substantially, even after her death in October 2014.

would feel for these higher vibrational beings to be around our much lower vibes.

The vast majority of the ETs Kiani has seen have been the little grey men, of course. They never came inside but just stood on the sidewalk in front of our house, looking up.

She's also seen what she calls "The Dog-head Aliens". These guys look like dogs but with human-like bodies. The ones she's seen resemble a combination of the golden retriever and the cocker spaniel. They like to look through windows and then scamper off when you try to see them better.

As I mentioned in my first book, she's also seen a "Reptilian", which is one of the more aggressive-natured extraterrestrials, from what I've read. They look like walking crocodiles or lizards.

One day, after my writing had started to reach a lot more people, she saw one with a cat head (this one walked right into our house and snooped around). Again, I looked this one up and found it.

The feline extraterrestrials are supposed to be an insatiably curious and creative race. They like to visit places where unusual, creative projects and ideas are being discussed and constructed and which also possess potential to cause great change.

So, I guess the fact that one was snooping around our house was actually quite the compliment!

We've also experienced something else that I've been told falls into this category, but truly, I'm no expert, so take it with a grain of salt.

The idea is that extraterrestrials keep tabs on people they think have potential for doing notable things, and they let you know you're being observed sometimes by tapping gently on objects around you *exactly* three times. (Some people say this is something regular spirits do and not just extraterrestrials, so I'll let you decide.)

This *three taps* phenomena has happened to us a few times, and it has all been on glass objects.

The most startling example of this happened while Kiani and I were out shopping. We had just finished, and I was backing the car out of the parking space when someone or some*thing* knocked on my window. The sound was unmistakable. Three solid knocks.

I immediately put my foot on the brake and turned to look, expecting to see someone standing there. Maybe I had dropped my wallet, or a friend had spotted us. But there was no one around.

Kiani was as baffled as I was and saw nothing out of the ordinary.

We commented on how strange it was and then I went back to maneuvering out of the parking lot.

I was just getting ready to turn onto the main street when we heard the knocking again, this time a little softer.

"All right, I hear you," I said, turning onto the street which would lead us home. "Are you in the car with us right now?" I asked.

I glanced at Kiani, who was looking into the backseat.

"You see anything?"

"Nope," she replied. "Feels like something is there though."

I tried again.

"Is there someone here who knocked on my window? Can you do it again, please?"

Nothing happened for a few seconds, then came the sound of three gentle taps behind me, very similar to the sound of someone tapping on glass with their fingernail.

After that, all went quiet. We never did find out what it was, but I thought it was fascinating.

As interesting as all these experiences were, the last extraterrestrial encounter of this book truly shocked us. Because of how profound the experience was, I decided it deserved its own chapter, so we'll come back to that in a little while.

2. WEIRD-LOOKING SPIRITS

The vast majority of spirits that Kiani sees are actually outside of our home, usually seen on the streets or in front of houses while I'm driving.

She distinguishes spirits from regular people by a few factors: If she can see through them, if they are in shadow form, or if they vanish into thin air while she's looking at them.

Sometimes, she knows them by what they're wearing, like old-fashioned clothing, heavy coats in the summer, and tank tops and shorts in very cold weather.

The solid-form, vanishing ones are the most common.

She knows I enjoy hearing about them, so when she happens to catch sight of one, she usually lets me know.

Most of them don't look unusual in any way, but occasionally, she will see some really weird things.

One example is a group of boys she saw standing just inside a house window.

There were five of them, all lined up in a row, staring outside. They were as still as statues, arms by their sides, each identical to the other with the exception of different-colored shirts.

Another time, after experiencing an increase in her abilities (preteen hormones), she saw a man dressed as a plague doctor (the doctors from medieval times, who treated plague victims behind birdlike masks filled with herbs and flowers to ward off the illness). He would show up when she was feeling overwhelmed and seemed to give off a feeling of peace wherever he was. I pulled a few tarot cards on this spirit and got the impression that he was watching over her and only appeared in this form because he knew it would make her laugh (which it did).

Other spirits that fall under weird, I suppose, would be the ones with only one limb. No body at all. Just an arm, for example. She says the arms most often materialize in mid-air and often do things, like try to pet our animals.

The creepiest ones (she made sure I included this) are when the arm emerges out from behind or under furniture. She says they are always children's arms. One even reached up from behind a bed and grabbed her shoulder.

Another time, my daughter encountered two very strange spirits within an hour. It happened one night when my mother was hosting a church party at our home. Around thirty people showed up this time, which added up to quite a lot of human energy and perhaps a spirit attachment or two. The first was a creature that very much resembled a starving "hobbit". It was around four feet tall, with a bald head and stooped shoulders. It was grotesquely thin, with white, almost transparent, shiny skin that stretched taunt over its bony frame. It stood facing partially away from Kiani and stared woefully into space, as if lost in thought and completely unaware of its surroundings.

The second one made my daughter laugh. It was a pair of human legs in grey trousers, three feet above the floor. No body. No head. Just the legs. She said she looked up to see it running across her room and into a wall, where it vanished entirely.

I almost fell over laughing when Kiani stood up and mimicked how the spirit had moved, "high-stepping" across the room, like a proud show pony in a hurry.

3. THE WEIRD, DARK ONES

We don't come across many dark spirits, mainly because we keep our home cleansed and blessed. But when we do and Kiani sees them, it can be rather disturbing, to say the least—especially when they look or behave in strange ways.

One time, she saw a completely black arm and hand reaching straight up through the floor before it vanished.

That same day, she also saw a black orb fly past her face in the bathroom. She's used to seeing a *lot* of orbs but had never seen a black one before. This one was also unusual in that instead of disappearing into the wall next to her, it actually hit the wall and made a *thunk* sound before vanishing.

The last one I mention gets *both* the scariest and weirdest award.

One day, she saw what looked like a little girl in a long, white nightgown standing outside our front door (this was before we learned to bless our property as well as our house). The girl's skin was as white as her nightgown, and she leered at Kiani with her face pressed up close to the glass.

When Kiani looked directly at her, she was startled to see that the girl's eyes were as dark as pitch, and her mouth was abnormally large. It was stretched into a snarling grin, with plenty of thin, sharp, pointed teeth, a bit like an evil version of the Cheshire cat.

Of all these strange and sometimes scary things, I would say the extraterrestrials are the most fascinating and most welcome of the bunch, as you'll probably agree.

I have a feeling we'll have many more encounters with aliens over the years, which is fine with me as long as we aren't "invited" up for an alien implant party. Yikes.

—CHAPTER 15—
THE GHOST GIRLS

You might think that the majority of ghosts can be found in old, abandoned buildings and cemeteries, but this isn't actually the case.

While earthbound spirits (ones who haven't crossed over) have an energetic connection with their physical remains/grave and favorite locations and can often sense when someone might be near these locations, the majority of them don't spend their time there.

Why? Because there are no people! Spirits get their energy from living humans. When they don't have it, they become lethargic and can even go into a hibernation-like state.

And since their energy source comes from humans, a large majority of them are drawn to highly populated locations.

Shopping malls, festivals, concerts, doctor's offices, government buildings, hospitals, and airports are a few examples. These places provide a delicious and varied energy buffet from which to choose from. When the spirit finds someone they like the look of or whose energy is especially appealing, they will often follow them home for a short or extended visit.

I imagine it might be a bit like a stroll through a candy shop for the energy-hungry ghost.

"Oh, wow! Look at them all! What do we have here? Angry teenager... depressed man...obnoxious woman... happy child... hmm... Oh, how about this one? Oh, I like this energy. It kind of reminds me of mine."

This was precisely how my sister, Deanna, who came to visit us for a few weeks, wound up at our front door with two ghosts right behind her.

The first night was the most intense. Spirits who've been in public locations *always arrive fully-charged and pumped full of energy.*

The first ghost, a preteen girl, was throwing out so much of her presence that I connected with her while sleeping.

In my dream, she was bouncing around my room, pointing out objects and demanding to know what they were, why I had them, and what she thought of them. It was exhausting me, even in my sleep. I forced myself awake and indeed felt a presence there with me.

Knowing full well that I would never get a good night's sleep if I didn't confront her, I stood up and lit some sage.

"Look," I said out loud, "I know you're hyper right now, but you're being rude. I'm trying to sleep, and I can't with you acting this way."

I waved the sage smoke around my bedroom and into my living room.

"Go outside and calm down a bit, okay? When you're calm, come back in if you'd like, and I'll help you if you need it."

I tamped out the smoke and headed back to my room, but no sooner had I got there when I heard the district sound of the front door lock being opened.

I went downstairs, and sure enough, it had been unlocked.

(It occurred to me that the new lock, which had been installed a week before, was electric and therefore much easier to manipulate than a regular one, since ghosts are "electrical" beings themselves.)

My opinion is that the girl was so excited to be here, she actually forgot she was only in spirit and tried to leave out the front door, like anyone would.

I didn't have long to wait in regards to the second spirit. Kiani sensed her the following day.

When I told her what had happened the night before, she closed her eyes and concentrated.

"Oh, yes, we have visitors," she said. "Two of them. I feel the girl you mentioned... and the second one is younger... maybe five years old... and she has red hair, like aunt Deanna."

Having now identified our newest visitors, we then sat down and tried to help them, as is our habit now.

First, I spoke out loud and called in The Great Spirit, our spirit guides, and spirit guardians (angels), requesting their help. Then I asked that the spirit children's family and friends be brought forward to speak to them from inside the light. Lastly, we focused our energy on visualizing a doorway of light for as long as we felt necessary.

It worked, as it usually does. Both girls left and never returned.

A couple months later, another girl showed up, which didn't surprise me. I'm now in the habit of specifically asking my guides and guardians to allow lost child spirits into the home that need help.

The first thing we noticed with this spirit was a sense of humor. On a couple occasions, when Kiani or Hap would step outside the front or back door (to water the plants or let the dog out), the door would lock by itself. Kiani was able to get back in easily enough because the front door is electric and she knows the code, but Hap had to knock to be let back in through the regular back door, which had us chuckling.

We wondered about this but didn't have an idea who it was until Kiani saw the full-form figure of a girl sitting on my bed, watching me meditate.

"She had long, dark brown hair to her waist," Kiani told me. "She looked like she was maybe twelve or thirteen. Normal clothes."

"What was she doing?"

"Just watching you, like she thought you were doing something really interesting."

By the time I was done meditating, the girl was gone. I asked Kiani to keep an eye out for her so we could make the light for her. Little did I know, however, that it would actually be *me* who saw her next.

A week or so later, I was washing my hands in the bathroom when I saw someone in my peripheral vision move quickly past the stairs and into my bedroom. The sound of walking could be heard as well, as the floorboards creak a little upstairs.

I didn't think anything of it at first, but something inside me said I should pay attention to this, and I've learned to listen to my gut. I quickly dried my hands and went to ask both kids if they'd just walked past the stairs.

Hap was seated at his computer and turned to look at me with a baffled expression.

"Nope," he said, shaking his head. "Wasn't me."

I quickly walked into my bedroom and found Kiani all cozied up under a blanket, playing with her tablet.

"No, but I heard someone walk in here," came her reply.

I pulled out my spirit box and Ovilus but didn't get anything that felt like real contact. I did hear the name "Rachel", but it was said in a man's voice. This was doubly odd to me because when I played the video back of the session, I couldn't hear it at all. Looking back on it, I suspect that my spirit guide might have been the one to speak, and the reason it didn't play back on the video was because I'd heard it in my mind.

In any case, it didn't matter too much. What was most important was helping her.

Instead of just making the light straight off this time, I contacted The Mystic Circle.

Years of connecting with people like myself online has resulted in me being very blessed in the psychic friend department. I call them "The Mystic Circle" because these ladies have incredible gifts. They have all been seeing and interacting with spirits since a young age. Listening to them talk about their experiences in a group chat is fifty times better than any ghost show!

"I just saw my third ghost!" I told them.

Immediately, two of the ladies honed right in on "Rachel".

"I feel like it's a child spirit," Narressa replied.

"Yes, definitely," said Karen.

"She's there because of you," Narressa went on. "You make her feel safe. She misses her parents though. I feel so sad for her."

"Poor girl! Okay, I'm going to make the light for her," I responded back.

"Okay... Aww! She just showed me a picture of her hugging you."

I almost teared up over that but quickly turned my focus to creating the light and calling her family forward.

This one was intense. Powerful waves of goose-bumps hit my body, traveling in a wave up my spine and across my scalp. When I was done, the energy felt different.

"I don't feel her anymore," Narressa said. "I think she's gone."

I felt both relieved and sad to see her go. I wish I could have seen the happy reunion with her family with my own eyes, but for now, I'll just have to im-agine it.

—CHAPTER 16—
THE WATER SPRITE

One of my favorite crystals (though I think it's more of a stone) is staurolite. It is also known as the fairy cross, fairy stone, or Cherokee cross.

There is something about the stone that is supposed to attract friendly nature spirits (fairies) of all kinds and to aid in communication with them. They are also known for other qualities and have been used as luck charms and talismans of protection for hundreds of years. The U.S. presidents Wilson, Harding, and Roosevelt were said to have worn them in their pockets.

There are many legends about where they came from. My favorite, of course, is a story about my tribe, the Cherokee.

One morning, a Cherokee village awoke to a troubling feeling in the air. The sky had turned grey and a terrible sadness came with it.

Soon, other villages joined together, and there was much talk about what it could be.

Suddenly, *The Little People (Yunwi Tsunsdi)* appeared from the edge of the forest. These fairy folk were said to be two feet tall, with beautiful, long black hair. They spoke first to the tribal elders and then to everyone assembled.

The Little People's story was both amazing and sad. They told of how years ago, a new star appeared in the Eastern sky, in a land beyond the ocean.

They said a boy-child of great wisdom had been born, who had been chosen by The Creator to teach his tribe about peace and healing.

He was a man of great kindness and brought strong healing medicine to his people. Even though his message was one of harmony and purity, he had many enemies who refused to hear his message of peace. They did not believe that his medicine could heal or that The Creator had sent him.

And so, on this dark day, this wise man would be tortured and killed by his tribe and cross over to the land of the spirits.

The Cherokee people were greatly saddened by

this news and began to cry for this wise man. Soon, all the animals came as well, and their eyes also filled with tears. The ground was covered in them.

When their crying finally stopped, the crowd looked down and discovered that their tears had transformed into little stone crosses.

The people gathered them up and kept them close to them, to honor the wise man who had died teaching the ways of The Creator.

1. *A photograph of a fairy cross, also known as a Cherokee cross*

It is interesting to me that, though I grew up in California, I wound up here in North Carolina, where my Cherokee family originated—and where many of *the Little People* were said to live.

Perhaps The Great Spirit wanted to bring me closer to my roots while teaching me so many new things. I may find out more one day, but for now, I am just grateful for what I have learned thus far and for the recent knowledge (thanks to my daughter's gifts) that fairies *do*, in fact, exist.

And not always in the form you would expect.

One day, I was driving home from the store, with Kiani next to me in the passenger seat.

Kiani and I had opened a couple drinks. I had mine tucked between my legs, and she was holding hers.

Suddenly, I heard a loud *splash*. Assuming that Kiani had spilled her drink, I glanced over at her and saw her staring at me, wide-eyed, drink still held off to the side.

"Did you spill your drink?" I asked her, looking back at the road.

"No," she replied in a strange tone. "That was *not* me!"

I glanced at her again and saw that her clothing was dry.

"What *was* that?" I asked.

Still wide-eyed, Kiani explained that she'd seen a stream of brown-tinged water appear in mid-air between us, about four inches from the ceiling. It fell downward and hit the center compartment, then vanished, leaving no trace of wetness. She said her arm had been splashed in the process.

I was surprised and intrigued and asked her if

she had seen anything, but she shook her head.

A couple minutes later, back in our driveway, Kiani's gaze was drawn to the backseat floor, where she saw a tiny creature hiding behind the seat.

She described it as being about three inches wide and round, like a little ball. Its body was fluffy, resembling the under-feathers of a bird, and it had one regular feather sticking out one side, like a tail. She couldn't see its face.

The description reminded me a lot of the little creatures that the Skeksis ate for dessert in The Dark Crystal.

Many of Jim Henson's creatures were inspired by an artist named Brian Froud. I often wonder just how similar these creatures are to actual beings unseen. Supposedly, there are many dimensions alongside our own and not just the "realm of the dead".

As I sat there marveling over our encounter, I suddenly recalled that I had left one of my staurolite crystals in my car (right where the water had hit). I'm certain that the little "water sprite", as I started calling him, found himself drawn to my car for this reason.

When I asked my spirit guides what he could be,

I heard the word "creek", which was interesting to me since there *was* a small creek near our house.

We tried speaking to him but got no response, so we told him that he was welcome on our property and could come indoors too if he liked.

So far, he hasn't shown himself again, but one never knows *what* to expect our house.

—CHAPTER 17—
MAN'S BEST FRIEND

Imagine for a minute that you're a ghost.

You see a white doorway near you everywhere you go, but you're worried about what is on the other side, so you ignore it. After a few days, it goes away.

You try visiting your family and friends, but all it does it make you feel sad. You feel like there is no place for you anymore.

Unsure what to do next, you decide to do some exploring. At first, you feel kind of guilty walking into peoples' houses, but you can't help it. You feel tired and out of it when you're not around living people, but public places just don't appeal to you. You long for a peaceful environment and gentle people, like yourself.

After a while, you decide that as long as you act like a regular guest who has been invited, walking into peoples' homes should be okay.

One day, you find yourself in front of a house that seems brighter than the rest. When you look closer, you see a beautiful, golden glow around the edge of property.

Curious, you reach out and touch it. It feels solid and warm and impenetrable, but just as you start to pull your hand back, you are filled with a feeling of love, and your hand slips through the barrier.

Unable to resist the urge to explore, you step through it and approach the house.

The front door is closed, of course, but that doesn't matter. You can walk through solid objects now that you're dead. It doesn't feel good, and you avoid it if possible, but you suppose it's the price you pay for walking in uninvited.

Once inside, you notice how much lighter it feels. This would definitely be a nice place to hide out next time you see a spirit you don't like the look of.

You start to look around, drawn first to an interesting assortment of antiques, fossils, and Indian artifacts in the front parlor.

Next, you move into the kitchen, drawn this time to the pleasant glow from an aquarium on the counter.

A sound behind you catches your attention, and you turn to see a young girl standing in the doorway.

Her eyes lock on yours, startling you.

She can see me?

"Mommy!" the girl shouts cheerfully, turning toward the stairs behind her. "There's a bald man in the kitchen!"

***

My head snapped up at this, and whatever I was doing on my phone was instantly forgotten.

A grown-up ghost? Haven't had one of those in a while.

"Coming!" I called back.

I snatched my Ovilus device off the shelf, dropped my phone into my pocket, and walked quickly down the stairs.

"Where is he?" I asked Kiani.

She raised her hand and pointed to the center of the kitchen.

"What does he look like?"

"Solid form. White man. Bald with glasses. Button-down shirt and slacks."

I turned the Ovilus on and set it down on the counter.

"Hello, sir," I said to the kitchen. "I can't see you, like my daughter can. Is it okay if I take your picture? I have some friends who might be able to see you in a photograph. If that's all right with you, stand by this chair, okay?"

I grabbed a chair and set it in the center of the kitchen, then stepped back and took the photo.

I quickly sent it off to *The Mystic Circle,* and they confirmed what Kiani had seen.

"Would you like some help? How did you get here?" I asked the man.

The Ovilus went nuts and went on with a few words that sounded like he had died in a truck and something about his son.

I talked to him a bit about the light and made it for him, but nothing seemed to happen.

"Details," said the Ovilus.

"Just made a connection!" my friend Narressa messaged. "His name is John. He panicking right now. He won't go in."

Aww, poor guy!

I apologized to John for scaring him and gave him the details he was asking for. I explained what was in the light, that no one could force him, and that loved ones were waiting for him.

Narressa was busy doing the same on her end.

"He's ready now," she said.

This time, when I made the light, the Ovilus was silent. Goosebumps rose on my arms, and I held the visual for a while.

After a minute or so, Narressa messaged, "He's gone. His dog came and got him. I saw him walk through."

I felt both touched and sad at this—sad because there was no human soul he trusted enough to follow but so incredibly touched that The Great Spirit would send just the right friend to help him: his *best* friend.

—CHAPTER 18—
GHOST PETS

Of all the spirit activity we've had over the years, I would say our favorites are always the animals.

One day, Kiani came into my room with a big grin on her face.

"You won't believe what's following me around the house!"

"What?" I asked, setting my book down.

"It's one of those little munchkin cats! The ones with the short legs."

"Oh, really?"

"Yep! I keep seeing her running along behind me, and she *loves* to watch me scoop the litter box for some reason."

I laughed. I'd had a few cats over the years who'd been the same.

Feeling rather enchanted with the idea of a munchkin finding us (we've always wanted one ourselves), I asked her to keep me updated.

What was interesting to me was how at home it seemed here. It kept up with its playful antics around the house, acting much like a typical young cat would, even going so far as to plop down on the dog's bed and stretch out as if to say, *"What are you gonna do about it, dog?"*

If Muppet noticed, he never cared. Cats are gods in his mind.

One day, though, something remarkable happened that served to validate one of my theories on the spirit world and even the inspired titles of my books.

You might recall from *Ghosts Like Bacon* that I've often wondered if spirits really *could* eat the food humans offered them. They certainly seem to "come to life" over the subject, as evidenced by the increased responses heard over the spirit box (*"bacon, coffee, latte, bacon, cream, ketchup, bacon"*). There was even one smartass ghost who took one look at my '50s-style dining table and asked me when I planned to serve dinner.

I didn't have to wonder about this for much

longer because the little cat answered my question. We might not have caught it if my guides hadn't pointed it out!

One day, I was playing music through a little Bluetooth jukebox in my kitchen while Kiani sat at the table, absorbed in a project.

Suddenly, the music stopped, and I felt the urge to look at my watch. It read forty-four after, which is a meaningful number to me and often used by my guides to get my attention.

"What happened?" Kiani asked.

"It just stopped at forty-four after," I replied.

Kiani, now distracted, lifted her gaze to a little table near my bedroom and gasped.

"Mommy! The munchkin kitty is eating the cat food!"

"Are you serious?" I turned to face the table but, of course, saw nothing with my boring variety of standard eyeballs.

"Yes! She's actually eating it, like turning her head to the side and crunching on it and stuff!"

"I *knew* it!" I said, giving in to the urge to jump up and down, though only once, which felt slightly more dignified.

Kiani laughed at me anyway and said, "Now we

know why Luna [our elderly golden retriever who'd passed away last year] kept showing up when you brought out the dog treats. She actually ate the ones you set down for her!"

"Yep," I said. "This also proves that everything has a spirit double. That's why ghosts don't fall through floors and why they can sit on furniture."

Though the munchkin charmed the socks off me, I have to admit to being *truly shocked* over the next animal to visit us. The chance of such a thing happening is, in my mind, extraordinarily rare.

One night, I was standing in front of the house, waiting on Muppet to deliver his eight p.m. package, when I looked up and noticed an unusual-looking star. It appeared to be encircled by at least fifty other, much smaller stars.

I called Kiani out to look, and we stared in wonder as at least fifty more tiny stars came up from under the encircled one to join the rest.

I tried to get a film of it, but it didn't turn out, sadly. We were still pretty excited about seeing something like that though.

As we sat there, we heard a rustling sound from the bushes to our right.

When we looked that direction, I saw nothing,

but Kiani saw what looked to be a large, black fox. She said it sat down where it was and gazed up at the sky, as if studying the same thing we were.

When we headed back inside a little while later, it got up and followed us in, at which point Kiani realized that this was *not* a fox.

"It's smaller than a wolf but bigger than a fox," she explained, then grabbed her tablet and pulled up her art program. Her finger moved across the screen as she sketched. "Its fur is all black, and it

has a really long, fluffy tail and long ears. The ears point backwards a bit though, almost like a rabbit but not that long."

2. *Kiani's sketch of the fox-like creature she saw*

I watched, enthralled.

"What's weird about it though," she said as she moved her finger back up to the animal's head, "is that it's eyes are all white. No other color. Just white...and it has little horns on its head."

My mouth fell open at this.

"Horns? For real?"

She turned to look at me and laughed at the expression on my face.

"It's not from this planet, obviously. I mean, it might be from another dimension, but I feel like it's another planet. He's definitely dead though."

She stopped drawing, lost in thought for a minute, then said, "I also feel like he used to be someone's pet. He's really sweet and wags his tail a lot. He understood what we were looking at outside, so he's also really smart. I wonder how he got here?"

Finally coming out of my initial shock, I closed my mouth and replied, "I don't know. Maybe he was a stowaway on one of those UFOs we saw outside."

"Like a hitchhiker?"

"Yeah."

Later that night, the little fox-wolf jumped up on our bed and curled into a little ball by Kiani's feet, which seemed to validate Kiani's feeling about him being a pet.

Wherever he came from and however he got here, I'm definitely glad he chose to visit us for a little while.

—CHAPTER 19—
THE GIFT

On October 26, 2018, I experienced something that I never thought possible. It has changed my life profoundly, and I honestly can't think of a better story for topping this book off.

As mentioned in a previous chapter, I was somewhat familiar with extraterrestrials, thanks to my daughter, but I never thought I'd actually come face-to-face with one.

In the weeks and months leading up to the encounter, I had been throwing all my spare time into learning different healing modalities.

I have always had natural healing abilities. When I was twenty-two, I had a friend with endometriosis. She was often in such terrible pain, and it hurt me to see her this way. One day, on a whim, I put my hands on her stomach and tried willing the pain away. To both of our surprise, it worked!

I did it a few more times after that, but sadly, I became fearful of it. I did not know what it was and still was not free of the fear of the unknown that religion had given me.

It wasn't until 2011 or so that I started experimenting with it again and soon discovered that some people called it "Reiki".

My form was a little different than what others seemed to do though. My natural instinct was to visualize pulling pain out of the body in the form of a black, tar-like substance and then shaking my hands into the air to release it. When I tried the standard form of just holding the hands still and visualizing healing, white light, it didn't work as well.

Later on, I took some Reiki courses and got my first and second attunement. I didn't notice anything during the attunement, but I did notice that my hands became very warm afterwards, and when I tried the standard form, it worked!

After that, I started combining the two—pulling out the black, then putting my hands over the body and visualizing the healing light.

On top of the Reiki courses, I also started studying a form of acupuncture using light instead of needles. This is basically a little machine that is pre-programmed with homeopathic frequencies to stimulate cellular healing. It looks a bit like a laser light, and you shine it over the pressure points that coincide with the body's organs.

I set a goal to start a career in alternative healing by February 2020. I've been learning a lot, but it has been slow at times since I homeschool my kids.

Well, not long after setting this goal, I started asking The Great Spirit for help. I wanted to be the best I could be at healing, and the first thing I felt intuitively was that I needed to get my health in order. I felt strongly that a good healer must heal themselves first.

For years, I'd been eating a mostly organic diet low in meat, sugar, and dairy. I enjoyed beer but wasn't a big drinker, and I took a lot of vitamins regularly as well. I used to feel amazing and wasn't a bit overweight.

Unfortunately, due to the trauma around my divorce, my adrenals became exhausted, and once that happens, it can be almost impossible to rid yourself entirely of chronic fatigue. And to top that off, damaged adrenals can cause an increase in food sensitivities, which had definitely happened with me.

The food that used to cause stomach upset in the past now caused me to gain ludicrous amounts of weight very quickly. Soon, even some *healthy* food started having this effect. Every day was a battle to keep from gaining weight.

Then, one day, I noticed an odd, poking sensation in the area of my liver and gallbladder. I immediately cut out beer (though I didn't drink much to begin with, it was best to be safe) and then fat, which my nutrition-savvy mom had recommended. It didn't seem to make one bit of difference what I ate, but I *did* notice that the sensation only seemed to happen when I was stressed, worried, or angry.

It then occurred to me that it might be my emotions and past trauma that needed to be repaired and not my diet.

You see, most people aren't aware of how electrical we are. Our bodies are organic machines, pulsing with electric currents from one end to the other. We are so electrical that even the space around us pulses with energy (the aura/biofield).

Nikola Tesla once said, "If you want to find the secrets of the universe, think in terms of energy, frequency, and vibration."

It's not just physical matter that carries frequencies or vibrations. Sound, light, color, and emotions carry them as well. The lower the emotion (anger, sadness, etc.), the harder it is on the body.

When we carry negative emotions around with us, it affects our health. Since electricity travels so well in water, and we are made up mostly of water, this means our emotions are carried by our blood throughout our bodies and into our organs continually.

I realized at that moment that my remaining anger from my past was all being processed through my liver and gallbladder.

If I didn't find a way to heal my past, I could suffer serious health consequences.

I quickly made a plan and started sleeping with crystals known for emotional healing. I also started working with some healers in the area.

The Great Spirit helped me heal the most through this, however, by giving me some vital knowledge in the form of Claircognizance. I was standing in the sunshine one morning when my mind was suddenly filled with a new understanding, as if someone had uploaded something into my mind instantaneously.

All of your kind and loving care toward other beings, though sometimes unappreciated or never returned, always *winds up back in the arms of The Creator, who returns it to you—especially if you are open to receiving it. In other words, your efforts are* never *for nothing.*

A major weight lifted at this point. I sat down and had an inner monologue with myself, asking the part of me that was angry to let go.

It worked. The pain in my side eased greatly, and even my remaining sad dreams vanished.

What I didn't know was that The Great Spirit wasn't done helping me heal.

One day, I was at a metaphysical store with a friend, who wanted to gift me with a crystal. I held my hands out and felt the air around me until I felt pulled in a direction.

It led me to a celestite crystal, which has high vibrations and connects you with higher beings. When I picked it up, I immediately noticed that the light blue crystal looked a lot like an alien head, with one big, cat-like eye. I felt I had to have it.

Later, back at home, and on a whim inspired by the alien-shaped crystal, I decided to try a little meditation video I saw on YouTube. Its intention was to help you remember what type of extraterrestrial you once were (I'm told we have had hundreds of lives on many planets). I went in with an open mind but not really expecting much.

When the lady in the video started listing a few extraterrestrial races, I felt the energy field around my body flex and tighten when she said the word *"Arcturian"* (this flexing sensation is also how I know which tarot cards to pull).

I didn't think too much of this yet, but when she asked what my job was in that lifetime, the word *"teacher"* jumped into my mind.

This baffled me. I've never felt drawn to that job (teaching my two kids at home is hard enough!), but then I realized that my writing *was* a form of teaching, which I *did* feel drawn to.

Just then, I saw an image in my head, like a very old memory, of sitting low to the ground and surrounded by children. Along with that came the knowledge that they needed to sit close to me in order to learn better; the energy of my aura helped open and activate their learning abilities.

Intrigued with what I'd experienced, I closed out the meditation and looked up a video on Arcturians.

A few things immediately caught my attention in regards to these tiny ETs (most are said to be only three to four feet tall).

First, the beings' large, cat-like eyes. I have been drawing them by the hundreds without thinking my whole life.

Second, the blue colors of their skin. I always joked that I was secretly a little blue alien.

And finally, the biggest shock came when it talked about the Arcticians' auras. They said their aura colors determined which jobs they took on, and only individuals with purple shades in their aura (mine is indigo) were given positions teaching children.

This was fascinating to me because over the past few years, I've come to realize that my aura/energy has been, my whole life, a catalyst for personal growth and change. Peoples' lives change when they connect with me. Whether it's a new job, meeting the love of their life, or gaining new motivation in an area they previously struggled in, interesting things happen all the time. I used to joke that I was a walking rabbit's foot, but it's more than that. My energy sends people into quiet introspection, leading them on an inner tour of sorts in their minds about who they are and how they can grow and change as a spiritual being.

You might think that sounds great, but most people don't want to think about stuff like that. I've lost many friends over the years, who simply walked off without a word. Or, unable to figure out why they felt so disturbed around me, they would pretend to be heavily offended over something trivial and split. It didn't matter what these friends and I did together or what we talked about. The effect was always the same.

This phenomenon has happened far too often in my life for me to ignore, and I was finally coming to terms with it. I even starting looking for others like myself, who crave personal growth and knowledge, and it has paid off!

I was completely amazed but also unsure what to make of what I'd learned.

Not being one to just take on any bit of information without careful consideration and connection, I set it aside in my mind and asked The Great

Spirit to validate this for me, if this information was accurate.

I didn't have long to wait.

The following day, I was sitting in my bedroom, listening to music, when my skin suddenly erupted in goosebumps.

I remember thinking, *Goodness! This isn't THAT great of a song!*

A few seconds later, I looked up to see Kiani standing in the doorway, eyes wide.

"Mommy! There's someone in the kitchen!"

"What? There is?"

"Yes!" she replied. "A white doorway opened up, and this iridescent energy came out! It's short, like this..."

She held her hand above the floor at about three and a half feet.

"Mommy, it's not human. I feel like it's an Arcturian. A female."

Amazed, I stood up and walked into the kitchen.

When I approached the area where my daughter said the energy was, I felt a sensation I hadn't experienced before. The skin on my head started tingling and pounding, and I felt mildly light-headed.

"Hello, bright one," I said by way of greeting, though I had no idea *why* I chose those words. "Is it okay if I take your picture for my psychic friends, to help me connect to you?"

I felt she wouldn't mind, so I snapped a pic and sent it off quickly.

The response came even quicker.

"I see it!" Nancy exclaimed. Then, "Gift! It has a gift!"

I felt a gentle expectancy from the being in front of me and asked her to follow me into my bedroom. It is my *sacred space,* where I feel most protected.

When I turned and walked away, Kiani said, "She's following you! Her energy is so pretty, Mommy! It's like rainbows on a bubble."

I sat down cross-legged and turned my Ovilus device on.

"She's sitting down in front of you now," Kiani said.

"What can I do for you, bright one?" I asked. "Do you have something for me, like Nancy said?"

I drew a quick tarot card, which I placed on front of me. It was *the star.*

I also felt the urge to say, *Violet.*

"Can I call you Violet?" I asked her. No response, but I felt that she didn't mind.

"Prepare," said the Ovilus.

I felt the urge to hold out my hands and did so, palms up. Immediately, I felt the sensation of an energetic weight on my hands, as if she had placed her own hands on or above mine.

The pounding, tingling sensation on the skin of my head increased significantly, with the top of my head being the most intense. The light-headedness also increased and stopped just short of being uncomfortable.

"Whoa!" said Kiani, pointing at my hands. "The area above your hands just turned a violet color!"

I closed my eyes and focused on tuning into her for a few moments and then, just as suddenly as she had appeared, I felt her leave.

Kiani and I stared at each other in amazement.

"I wonder what she gave you."

"I don't know! Something good, I imagine!"

I didn't sleep well that night. There was an odd, heavy feeling in my chest, and I couldn't pinpoint it, which bothered me. I needed to talk to someone who had knowledge of Arcturians.

When I woke up the next morning, I was shocked to discover that I'd dropped three pounds. It's hard for me to lose weight with my food sensitivities and the state of my adrenal glands, and I'd even eaten ice cream the night before!

I posted in my metaphysical support group, asking about Arcturians. To my pleasant surprise, my friend, Liz, messaged me, asking if she could help since she was knowledgeable in this area.

When I told her what had happened, she connected quickly with her Arcturian guides, and the answers came to her.

"The gift you've been given is the gift of "violet flame" energy," she explained. "It is a gift of healing. Healing for you as well as the ability to heal others. It is an attunement of sorts—like Reiki but stronger."

I spoke to her about the uncomfortable feeling in my chest and asked her if she could do some healing on that area for me (many attuned healers can heal from a distance as well as in person).

"I don't understand why I'm feeling this way," I told her. "It feels like fear, but I wasn't afraid of Violet."

I told her that I thought it might be a purging of fears I've been carrying around, since purging is common after a healing.

She said she would love to help and would message me back.

Not long after, the tightness and fear in my chest vanished, and she messaged me.

"When I tuned into you, the Arcturians were already there, working on your heart area," she told me. "They showed me a vision of them reaching into your chest and removing a locked box. They took a spinning orb out of it and put it back in your chest without the box."

I was floored.

"Really? What is it?"

"The orb is part of your power and your direct connection with them. You can access it to aid you in healing, and it will give you answers. When you have questions, put your hand on your chest and ask them out loud, and you will feel the answer."

Wow.

Liz continued, "The orb has always been a part of you. You just didn't have access until now. The more you ask it questions, the clearer the answers will be, and you will trust it more. They are saying, '*Practice, practice, practice.*'"

Talk about a mind-blowing conversation.

I thanked her profusely, to which she replied with, "They did all the work! I just got to witness it!"

I didn't waste time in talking to them as Liz had instructed. To my intense pleasure, they answered back in the form of a *feeling of knowing* with each question I asked.

My eyes watered up, and my heart swelled with love.

"Thank you for the gift," I whispered. "I am so grateful."

A few days later, after noticing how the pain in my side had completely vanished and that I was continuing to lose weight, I ran a scan on my body through the BioLight machine. My liver and gallbladder levels were back to normal, and even my adrenal glands seemed to be functioning normally.

This was beyond anything I'd ever experienced. I have a feeling that whatever Violet gave me won't be fully understood for a few more years, but that's all right with me.

I am immeasurably content just knowing that it's not only our guardian spirits and The Great Spirit itself that loves us. We have a *whole team* of light beings working alongside us.

No matter what we've been through or how unsupported we feel at times, we need to remember that *we are loved... and we are never alone.*

—Part 3—
Tips, Tricks, and Light Rituals

—CHAPTER 20—
HOW TO PROTECT YOUR HOME AND FAMILY FROM NEGATIVE SPIRITS

(Revised and updated from the similar chapter in
Ghosts Like Bacon*)*

*T*his chapter is not just for families of psychic children. The protection techniques listed below work for anyone in need of them.

If you do have a child who sees spirits, however, I can't stress enough how vitally important it is to create a safe home environment for them; a place where they don't have to hide who they are; a place where they can gently develop and understand their gifts without fear of low-level spirits.

I want to remind you that these are my personal recommendations. They worked for us and continue to work to this day. Chances are, as you get to know your child and/or yourself and grow in knowledge both spiritually and energetically, you will come up with your own twist or take on other great suggestions from people with experience.

Most importantly, you must understand that you and/or your child are not alone and that everything will be okay!

God, The Great Spirit, love, the universe, etc. has a plan, and it does not involve you and/or your child being miserable.

Before I proceed with the light rituals and techniques below, I need to point out how important it is to take a moment to connect to The Source/The Creator before proceeding with the following. Whether it is home cleansing, severing a spirit connection, making the light for a spirit or any spirit work at all, it is vital that you first connect with The Source of love and light. This will ensure that you are protected and successful as well as help strengthen the bond between you and The Source in general.

To do this, stand or sit someplace comfortable, close your eyes, and take two deep breaths.

On the first breath and its exhale, imagine your legs as the roots of a tree. Visualize them growing down, down, down into the earth and attaching firmly there. This will ground your energy and keep your spirit strong during spiritual work.

On the second breath, visualize a window in the top of your head opening up. Pull the light of The Source down through this open window and into your body. Visualize your body and spirit filling up with pure love and light directly from The Creator.

You are now fully connected and ready to help yourself and others.

Step 1
CLEANSING YOUR HOME

What you need:

Faith (If you don't believe in a higher power, chances are you believe in *love,* so tap into it and use it.)

Intention (Take charge, speak with a strong voice, and mean what you say.)

A bundle of dried sage (Other herbs and in-gredients in your cabinet can do the trick in a pinch – vinegar, rosemary, cumin, dill, thyme, and basil leaves among them – but sage works extremely well and is easier to work with. Herbs work *wonders* for affecting energy and spirits. The Great Spirit knew exactly what he was doing when creating these plants.)

A bowl (to catch the ashes from the sage)

NOTE: If you own a Tibetan singing bowl, you can use this in the cleanse as well. I've found that the beautiful tones and frequencies of the bowls strengthen protective ceremonies.

Light the sage and blow it out to create a gentle flow of smoke. You may have to relight and blow out a few times throughout. Keep a bowl under it to catch any small sparks that fall.

Stand with the sage in the center of the house and say something along these lines (change the words to personally represent your beliefs and values, even if it's only using the force of love):

> *Father Spirit, Creator of Life and Love,*
> *draw close to this family.*
> *We are your children, Father,*
> *and we honor you.*
> *We ask that you bless our family*
> *and bless this house and this property.*
> *Remove all negative spirits from this*
> *home and block them from entering.*

Now address the spirits:

> *Spirits in this house, listen closely.*
> *This house and the family who*
> *live here are under the protection of*
> *The Father Spirit, The Creator of Life*
> *and Love. If you do not come here*
> *with love in your heart,*
> *then you are trespassing.*
> *Leave now and never return.*

These are strong words.

Anything negative in your home will immediately flee.

Repeat the last paragraph of the cleansing or a shortened version as you continue.

Now walk along each wall of the house and through the center of each room, pausing at each window and door. Trace the shape of them with the sage and visualize forming an impenetrable seal of light over each one.

For added benefit, you can also stand in your yard and visualize throwing white light out to the edges of your property and a bit beyond. But remember to always pull light or anything else you visualize down from The Source and into your body first.

When you return to where you started, tamp out the sage (much like a cigar) and take a deep, relaxing breath. You should feel a change in the energy of the house.

At this point, for added benefit, I like to hit the side of my singing bowl and visualize an impenetrable, armor-like bubble around my property.

Then I say something like this:

> *I now draw in the light of The Creator to strengthen the protective, golden armor around this property so that nothing harmful may enter. Let only those with love in their hearts be allowed onto this property and into this home. By the power of The Creator of life and love, this armor is now in place.*

I recommend repeating this ritual once every fifteen to thirty days. It will make a huge difference.

Step 2
BEDTIME CLEANSING

I recommend that you sage the bedrooms every night, right before bedtime. You needn't say too much—just a quick prayer of protection and request for a good night's sleep.

Extra safety tips:
Used objects: If you bring a used or crafted object into your home, run it through sage smoke. Objects can carry negative energy or spirit attachments that aren't welcome.

Salt lamps: I learned about salt lamps from a spirit medium. I recommend buying one to keep in each bedroom where it is needed. Low-level entities avoid them.

Herb mixtures: I also recommend placing or hanging bundles of herbs (I put mine in plastic balls from craft stores) in each room.

Here's an ingredients list that I found to be amazingly affective:

1 tsp dill

1 tsp cumin

1 tsp clove

1 tsp thyme

1 tsp basil

1 tsp rosemary

1 tsp cinnamon

1 bay leaf

A bit of dried sage

1 tsp periwinkle and lavender (if available)

Step 3
CRYSTALS

It is a scientific fact that every living being and inanimate object on this planet vibrates with a frequency of its own.

I often call crystals "medicine stones" because I believe that The Great Spirit gave each of them individual frequencies that can be used to help our bodies and minds in a variety of ways.

When you carry them close to your body, your body responds by trying to match its vibration with those of the crystal. In this way, bad vibrations can affect us as well. Ever notice how being around someone grumpy (even if they don't talk) makes you feel grumpy too? This is how frequencies and vibrations work. When you are aware of them, you are better able to decide what you keep near your body.

There are many crystals and stones that are beneficial to a child with special abilities, but here is a list of my favorites – the absolute *must-haves*. I recommend purchasing the crystals listed below and keeping them close to or on you always. Keep in mind that I only list *some* of their uses. To find out more, check online.

THE AMAZING FIVE

BLACK TOURMALINE

This stone is powerful. It sucks in bad energy and throws it back out as positive. On top of this, it also absorbs harmful EMF from electronics. It is a comforting stone, sucking up all your sadness and helping you to see the bright side. But most importantly for us, it protects from psychic attacks, from both humans and spirits.

I recommend keeping this stone in the pocket or

on the body always. Sleep with it by your head at night, if you can't wear it.

LABRADORITE

This stone protects the aura from the energy of humans and spirits. Being both an empath and an introvert, I never go anywhere without this stone. Even when I'm in a huge crowd, I'm never bothered or drained by others' energy, as I am without it.

Labradorite is especially wonderful for sleep. To me, it feels like someone shutting a door between me and a noisy party going on outside my room and then gently laying a fuzzy, warm blanket across me.

As I've mentioned before, I am also sensitive to spirits, and I've always felt especially vulnerable while sleeping. My guard is down, and for some reason, spirits think that two a.m. is a great time to talk.

One time, I forgot to wear it when I went to bed and was woken twice by the sound of a ghostly cat howling and a child's voice chattering happily in the next room. I grabbed my stone and bam! Peaceful silence.

SELENITE

This crystal has one of the highest vibrations. Hold it in your hand, and you'll often feel a little warm and tingly where it sits. It can both cleanse and charge your other crystals and needs no cleansing itself.

STAUROLITE

It protects against unwanted spirits, attachments, and negative influences. It also guards against fear, which is an attractive energy to many ghosts.

SPIRIT QUARTZ

This has a strong dampening effect on fear. It protects against unwanted spirits and helps to raise your body's positive vibrations, enhancing your natural ability to connect with angels and other light beings.

CLEANSING YOUR CRYSTALS

We don't just absorb crystal's vibrations; they absorb ours too. This is why cleansing them is important.

To do this, simply set them next to or on top of a selenite crystal, or light your sage bundle and run the crystal through the smoke a couple of times. Remember that selenite also charges the other crystals, which is a bit like giving them a great night's sleep, so they are ready to do their job protecting you.

In my home, I use selenite or a *VibesUp* mat (www.vibesup.com) for charging, which is like selenite times fifty. I also recommend buying one of their "Earth ION pyramids". Negative spirits hate them. They're awesome!

Black Tourmaline doesn't need charged as much as other crystals, but I still do it every week or two anyway. Labradorite needs it every few days, as does spirit quartz and staurolite.

Step 4
PERIWINKLE HERB

As mentioned in *Ghosts Like Bacon*, this herb made a huge difference with my daughter and myself.

(DO NOT EAT IT. I mean for you to *wear it.*)

From what we can tell, negative spirits are only

able to get about forty feet from the stuff. They don't like it *at all.*

Now, I'm not saying you won't sense them at a distance, but a distance is *way* better than up close. They will have a *much* harder time harassing a human from that distance.

If you keep your home cleansed on a regular basis, you shouldn't have any problems with negative entities. The periwinkle is an added protection and creates a "cleansed space" around your body, so it's especially important to wear it outside of your home. It keeps dark entities out of your body space and stops them from following you or your child home, which I've had experience with as well.

You can purchase vials and the herb online and make your own amulets or search for someone who sells them pre-made.

THE DARK ONES

This the term I use for the very dark spirits, often referred to as "demons". If whatever is in your house is causing a feeling of extreme fear, there is a good chance that this is what you're dealing with. These things can be much harder to get rid of. They are mean, stubborn and full of themselves. They may not be able to get into your home when it's sealed by The Source, but that won't always stop them from trying or even bullying you outside of the house. They have no right to do this.

If you encounter one of these awful beings, you can order them away by using the many names of The Source. But in my experience, it's better to call in Archangels/Elite Guardians immediately. Don't worry one second about "bothering" Archangels. It's not possible. They are multi-dimensional and omni-present. Aiding you is their mission, and they love to help. All you have to do is ask.

Any of them will come to help you when called, but my favorite and the very quickest to respond in this situation is Michael.

Visualize electric blue light and a mighty sword and say something like this:

Archangel Michael, please hear me and come quickly to my side. There is a Dark One threatening my family, and I need your help. Please take him away and do with him what you will. Thank you, Michael. I am grateful.

NOTE: *Metatron* is another good Archangel to call in with Michael if you have children. Metatron absolutely loves children and is very protective of them.

ONE FINAL NOTE

If you've done all the above and still feel a negative entity in your home, then chances are you have a spirit attachment, human or otherwise. It doesn't happen often, but it's not unheard of. There are energy cords that form between people we love, work with, and sometimes even just have an intense moment with. These invisible cords are formed by thoughts and emotions and can come from both people or just one. They can even form online, from a heated conversation.

You can learn more about these cords and how to cut the negative ones in the following chapter.

—CHAPTER 21—
HOW TO SEVER ENERGY CORDS AND SPIRIT ATTACHMENTS

When you think of hauntings, you think of houses, right? Well, people can be haunted as well (by both humans and spirits). There are invisible cords of energy that connect us to other people whom we've shared intense emotion with – and not just people we've met either.

Sometimes, cords can form from a heated or emotional conversation between two people online. Think back on your own online experiences. Have you ever been involved in some sort of a dignified debate with someone, and they suddenly turned vicious and lashed out at you? How did you feel afterward? Did you sleep well? Did it leave you with a disturbed kind of feeling? Did you keep thinking about it?

I think if people aren't careful to avoid angry people and drama in general, then one can become quickly "strung up" with cords of energy. They are all connected to you and your vitality, therefore affecting your energy levels, your peace of mind, your health, and even the health and peace of mind of the people closest to you, who are likewise connected to *you*. That's quite a tangle of cords, isn't it?

I believe an unexpected effect of these cord connections is that they can also act as spirit pathways between people. If that guy at work who yelled at you and called you names has a grumpy spirit of an old man attached to him, what's stopping that spirit sucking energy off *your* energy cord, which is now throwing out delicious hurt as the result of the name-calling? Your cord is now attached to his favorite human, after all. Fair game!

Cords or spirit attachments between spirits and humans can be the most harmful of them all. Psychics, spirit mediums, and people suffering greatly from mental illness can be especially vulnerable to spirit attachments, if they are not careful to keep a strong and steady connection to The Light (the source of love), both within their homes and within themselves.

We can't always stop these cords from forming (though I have discovered that wearing black tourmaline or black obsidian can stop most negative ones), and some of them are beneficial, like the ones to your children and loving family members. Ever wonder why you feel so connected sometimes? How they call you right when you think of them?

But we can start by being aware of the cords. Once you are, then the next logical step would be careful consideration when it comes to who we choose to bring into our lives and how we choose to connect with strangers, family, clients, coworkers, etc. Keep your vibes up! Choose your words carefully, and let nothing come from your mouth that does not come from love.

Every negative word from you and every negative action has a dark reaction. It fills your spirit with darkness and pushes out the light, which is our only true protection.

Emotions, thoughts, and intentions are powerful. You can cut a toxic person out of your life or drive a spirit entity off your property and into the setting sun, but if your energy is especially appealing to a negative person or an entity, the cord can sometimes stay attached. It can affect your sense of peace, your mood, and your focus and if it's a spirit attachment you're dealing with, it can be especially clingy, making it hard to just relax and be your happy self.

Here is a simple technique for cutting energy cords:

Sit by yourself somewhere, close your eyes, and visualize the sky above you opening up and spilling down intense, love-filled, white light. See yourself completely covered in it. Take deep breaths and breathe in the white light.

Next, visualize each positive loved one's cord attached to you and gently set them aside to your left or right. Then take a piece of selenite or just your hand and visualize holding a flaming, hot, white and blue sword or knife. Visualize and even mime cutting around your body, leaving your loved ones' cords untouched at your side. See in your mind the unwanted cords snapping, breaking, and shriveling off from your body, like burning hair or rope fibers. Pay the most care at the front of your body, near the stomach, and your back.

Once that is done, smudge your body the best you can with some dried sage and take an Epsom or sea salt bath if possible.

This technique works well in the majority of situations, but sometimes, a cord or spirit attachment that has been around a long time or is particularly dark in nature can be harder to remove. If this is the case or you feel that it might be a bit more serious, then I would consider blessing your body, much like you would your house.

Here is how I came up with the idea:

Kiani's best friend is a little girl named Melissa. Kiani asked me to help her one day because Melissa was being stalked by something dark. It had been going on for a couple years, and Kiani had been able to validate Melissa's experiences and feelings on it, having been to her house. When Melissa would visit us, the dark spirit would split, but once back home, it went back to following her around, trying to make her feel afraid.

I told Kiani I would definitely help her and pulled out a piece of paper. I wrote down some words to use in the ritual for severing a spirit attachment and used it the next time she came to our house.

The effect was immediate. The spirit left and never returned.

Here is a copy of the ritual I wrote. Feel free to use it to help yourself and others. You can also rewrite parts of it to better represent your personal beliefs in regards to The Source. It will immediately and effectively sever all spirit attachments AND negative energy cords.

I recommend smudging the body with sage afterwards, followed by an Epsom salt bath, if possible.

Blessing a Living Being

Father Spirit, Mother Earth, Spirit Guides, and Guardians of the living souls in this room, I ask that you draw close to us and assist us.

I bless this body and its spirit, known as _____, in the name of The Great Spirit, The Creator of Life and Love. I fill this body with pure, white light directly from the source of love. By the power of The Great Spirit, I now sever all dark energy, harmful energy cords, and low-level spirits attached to this body and the spirit within.

Stop here and run selenite or a black crystal an inch or two away from the body, starting from where the legs meet, up the front of the body, to the top of the head, then down the neck to the top of the back. From there, move the crystal around the waist a couple times.

> *Dark spirits and negative energy now formerly connected to _____, hear my words. This living being belongs to The Great Spirit, the creator of life and love. You no longer have any connection to this human soul. You are cast aside. LEAVE NOW AND NEVER RETURN.*

—CHAPTER 22—
HOW TO HELP AN EARTHBOUND SPIRIT INTO THE LIGHT

Do you have a ghost in your home?

If you don't want it there, you may think you are helpless to do anything about it, but that is far from the truth. It is your home, your space, and your body, and you *absolutely* have a choice about what you allow in that space. You don't need outside help either. If you want them removed, *you can do it all on your own and with the help of your angels and Spirit guides.*

If you don't mind the ghost being there, then let it be, but you do need to be aware of a couple things first.

1. **Every Spirit has its own energy**, just like when they were alive. Some spirits are kind, happy,

silly, or playful, while others are depressed, angry, resentful, and controlling.

Earthbound spirits don't need sleep or food, but they *do* need energy to function, and the *only* way to get it is from living humans.

(*What about electronics?* Nope. Spirit energy is perfect for manipulating electronics, but they don't get energy from them.)

Whatever energy the spirit possesses is what they need to recharge. If they're depressed, they feed off sad emotions from humans. If they're angry, they look for angry emotions. If they are hateful, they feed off hate. If they are controlling or crave power, they feed off fear.

Because they need and crave these emotions, they can and often *will* try to induce these feelings in living humans to meet their energy needs.

What's terrible about all this is *it isn't free.* We, as living humans, pay for it. When our energy is taken by these spirits, it drains us and messes with our natural emotions as well as our immune systems. We will feel exhausted, depressed, irritable, and afraid. And because our immune systems are affected, we can get sick much easier, even so far as developing a variety of more serious health problems.

(One bit of good news in all this is that the cheerful, kind ghosts don't seem to have this draining effect, which, to me, really points to the healing aspect of positive emotions. Regardless, we do need to understand how these energies affect us.)

2. It may not have occurred to most people, **but these spirits have places to be and things they need to be doing in the afterlife**, and I can assure you that *your living room is not it.*

Before a spirit crosses over into the light (where their family and loved ones are waiting), they are considered to be earthbound. This is a highly fitting phrase to me because they might as well be bound up or even tied up. They are not moving on with their destiny (whatever The Source, Angels, or The Great Spirit has planned for them).

3. **Every spirit has free will.** The light is there for them to walk through from the second they leave their body to about seventy-two hours after their funeral. (See Mary Ann Winkowski's writings in *As Alive, So Dead: Investigating the Paranormal* and *When Ghosts Speak: Understanding the World of Earthbound Spirits.* If you haven't read

her books, you're missing out!) If they don't walk through, then they must find the light elsewhere by finding another newly deceased person with the light behind them or someone willing to create the light for them.

They can walk through this light any time they want to, *but the choice is theirs. You cannot force them into it.*

That being said, it's my belief that most spirits who refuse to go into the light make this choice because they are *afrai*d. They don't know what is waiting for them there.

I do, however, have a great sense of inner-knowing and peace about what is in The Light, which was what gave me the idea of the perfect way to help these spirits. It has worked very well for my daughter and me.

Before following the technique below, keep in mind that *you do not have to help them if you feel uncomfortable doing so*, particularly if the spirit is a mean one. If this is the case, I would recommend following the instructions in the protection chapter and removing that thing from your house.

Now onto making The Light...

1. Set a dried sage bundle next to you, but don't light it until the very end or if you start to feel overwhelmed.

2. This is optional, but if you're new to visualizing things, light a candle and set it in front of you. I'll explain why in a bit.

3. Now call in or pray for your personal light beings to be with you (The Source, God, The Light, love, angels, spirit guides, guardians—whichever resonates with you). Tell them about your intention to help the spirit in your home, and ask that they reach out for and find the family and loved ones of the earthbound spirit. Ask them to bring these loved ones forward from the light, to speak with the spirit in your home while you focus on creating The Light for them.

(When my daughter and I first started making The Light, we didn't think to bring their loved ones forward. The spirits would remark over the appearance of The Light, and some *did* walk through, but most stayed, which we found frustrating. Bringing their loved ones forward made a tremendous difference!)

4. Now close your eyes (or stare into the candle flame if you're new to visualizing) and focus on visualizing a door appearing in the room. Make it as bright white as you possibly can. *See it* in your head. Put all of your intention and focus into this. ***Think of nothing else but this doorway of light!***

Then *hold this visual* for a least a couple minutes to give your angels, spirit guides, etc. time to do what you asked them to.

While this is happening, you may experience a few sensations, like goosebumps or ringing in your ears. Or you may not feel much of anything. It's all normal. Keep focusing.

What the earthbound spirit in your home will see is a bright doorway suddenly forming. Someone who is important to them will step through it and toward the spirit. The spirit will recognize them, and there will be a brief and loving conversation, usually with a lot of hugging and some happy tears. Then they will turn and walk through the light with their loved one.

Again, there may be cases where the spirit refuses to go, as is their choice, but it doesn't happen often. The important thing is that you're giving them the opportunity, and it's an amazing one.

You may also feel the moment when the spirit leaves because the energy of the room will feel very light, quiet, and still. Whatever was there is now gone.

5. When you're all done, go ahead and light that sage bundle and smudge the house to clear out any residual energy... and enjoy your ghost-free home!

Well, at least for a little while... before the smell of fresh-brewed coffee and sizzling bacon—or whatever else ghosts seem to like—glides past the nose of your next ghostly visitor.

At least now you know what to do.

May The Source be with you,
Sam

—ABOUT THE AUTHOR—

Samantha Red Wolf started writing at age ten, but nothing felt right until she wrote *Ghosts Like Bacon* and its sequel, *Ghosts Like Coffee*. She hopes that her stories will go a long way toward helping families like her own. Sam is currently studying for a career in alternative medicine, but in her free time, she enjoys reading, painting, playing and practicing the acoustic and bass guitar, and being a big kid as much as she can get away with.

Samantha lives in North Carolina, USA with her two kids, her best friend (mom), and their many spoiled animal friends.

You can find her on Facebook at **face-book.com/samantha.redwolf.9**.

The first book of this series, *Ghosts Like Bacon*, can also be read in blog format at:

www.ghostslikebacon.com.

Made in the USA
Lexington, KY
17 December 2019